ADVANCE PRAISE

"Extensively researched and well-written, [the book] quickly engrosses the reader into a sad chronology of frightening events, intertwined with many historical facts, during the Holocaust, and its aftermath. As a Holocaust survivor, I can attest that this book is a tour de force for anybody interested in history."

—Alter Wiener, death camp survivor and author of *From a name to a number. A Holocaust Survivor's Autobiography*

"I was very impressed with how this book resonated with history. I really cared about the characters and wanted to see how life worked out for them. As I read the book, I found myself feeling like a fly on the wall, fully immersed and involved in its content. It would make a spellbinding movie."

—Jean Perloff, Attorney at Law

"Terrific book. I couldn't put it down. I kept reading and reading until I finished it a few days later. I enjoyed the characters and the action. I like that the writing was simple and direct, not full of side trips and flowery language. It's a real page-turner."

—Jeffrey Wood, founder of AudioHighway.com

"The story speaks of a time that changed the future path of millions of innocent families, and how some survived only on threads of hope and kinship. The story makes you think—as it should: Never again! I highly recommend *The Precious Few* to any reader interested in the human tragedy we know as the Holocaust."

—Wayne R. Bayliff, author and publisher

"Instead of dwelling on the dark horror of Holocaust events, the Precious Few focuses on the uplifting bravery and heroism of disparate young Jews who challenged the powerful Nazi stranglehold and succeeded, each in their own way. It left me feeling greatly moved."

—Claire Kahane, PhD, professor emerita, and author

THE PRECIOUS FEW

AN INSPIRATIONAL SAGA OF COURAGE
BASED ON TRUE STORIES

DAVID TWAIN
ART TWAIN

ISBN 9789493322035 (ebook)

ISBN 9789493322011 (paperback)

ISBN 9789493322028 (hardcover)

Publisher: Amsterdam Publishers, The Netherlands

info@amsterdampublishers.com

The Precious Few is part of the series Holocaust Books for Young Adults

Copyright © Art Twain, 2023

Cover image: Collyn Vargo

All Rights Reserved. No part of this publication may be reproduced or transmitted in any form or by any means, electronic or mechanical, including photocopy, recording or any other information storage and retrieval system, without prior permission in writing from the publisher.

CONTENTS

Prologue	1
1. AVRUM	3
I am Avrum	3
My Beginnings	4
Our Village	5
Shabbos Dinner	6
Young Avrum	8
Protecting Lena	9
The Next Day	11
The Train Ride	13
2. LENA	15
The Kwalskis	15
Hiding	16
Germans	18
Mother Superior	19
The Convent	20
Irena's Secret	22
The Gestapo	24
After the German Visit	26
Anna	27
Anna's Story	29
Lena's Thoughts	31
To the Forest	31
The Partisans	33
The Partisan Camp	35
3. MOLLIE	38
Mollie	38
On the Farm	40
Meeting the Partisans	42
4. AVRUM	44
Day after Day	44
The *Kapo*	46
We are the Jews	48

The Tailor	50
Talking with the Colonel	52
The Colonel	54
5. LENA	**56**
Chaya's Story	56
The Escape	58
Staying Alive	60
Farmer Janusz	61
The Jewish Partisans	63
Back in Camp	64
The Train	66
After the Sabotage	67
6. AVRUM	**70**
To Camp	70
Returning to Camp	71
Itzhak	74
Discussion with Itzhak	75
Mendel	76
The War Wears On	78
7. LENA	**81**
The Twerskis	81
The Other Partisans	83
Planning The Raid	85
The Raid	88
After the Raid	95
In the Forest	96
We Need Supplies	100
The Air-Drop	102
Plan in Action	104
The War Ends	106
8. AVRUM	**108**
Liberation	108
The Day After	110
Returning Home	111
The Mission	112
Looking for Lena	113
Returning from Leszno	117
Recuperating	120

9. MOLLIE	122
The Warning	124
The Russians Arrive	125
Having to Leave	127
Traveling with the Palestinians	130
10. LENA	133
We Move On	133
Making Plans	135
Before the Journey	137
The Journey	139
The Service	142
Crossing the Border	143
To Bergen-Belsen	146
Arriving at Bergen-Belsen	147
Preparing for Our Next Life	149
11. MOLLIE	152
Feldafing	152
12. AVRUM	155
Finding a Friend	155
Mollie and Me	157
Looking for Mollie	159
Getting Married	162
Yankel Leaves	163
To America	166
The Voyage	167
America	170
Being Americans	173
We Settle In	175
13. COMING TOGETHER	178
To Palestine	178
The Ship	181
Sailing to the Promised Land	183
The Promised Land	187
14. FINALITY	189
Understanding the Situation	191
Canada	193
Mandate Ends	195

Mohamed Ali Hadad	198
Yad Mordechai	199
15. NEW WORLD, NEW LIFE	**204**
Cleveland, 1962	204
Events in Cleveland	205
Josh's Bar Mitzvah	207
Teaching Class	209
Our Son, Solly	213
16. AVRUM AND JACOB	**215**
At the Park	215
Epilogue	217
Acknowledgments	219
About the Authors	221
Amsterdam Publishers Holocaust Library	223

PROLOGUE

The Jewish Experience in Poland

The first Jews came to Poland in approximately 966 AD. They filtered in over the years, their population increasing at a steady rate. Then, after the year 1492, there was a marked jump as the Spanish Inquisition forced Jews to leave Spain if they refused to convert to Catholicism. Emigration gained momentum when, some years later, antisemitism drove the Jews out of Austria, Hungary, and Germany. Many searched out their brethren in Poland.

While the environment in Poland wasn't perfect for Jews, it was an improvement over the conditions in Spain. Fifteen years passed before the next group of Jews arrived from Italy and Turkey. By the middle of the 16th century, three quarters of all Jews in Europe lived in Poland. About 50 to 70 percent of the Jewish population in Poland lived in smaller towns and villages. They remained Jews in spite of enormous antisemitic pressure, much of which was fostered by the Catholic Church.

In 1931, the Jewish population in Poland totaled 3,130,000. By 1939, it had grown to 3,474,000. In Warsaw alone there were 375,000 Jews: approximately half the population of the city. Due to laws that deprived Jews of land ownership and of reaching higher positions in government, the military, and business, Jews focused their efforts on selling and money handling. As a result, they excelled in the retail business, which produced many wealthy Jewish merchants. There was also an unusually high percentage of Jewish teachers, journalists, and lawyers. In addition, 56 percent of the doctors in Poland were Jewish.

As the Jewish community prospered all on its own, envy of Jewish success and antisemitism grew in parallel. Those negative attitudes had reached an uncomfortable peak when, on September 1, 1939, Germany declared war on Poland and, more specifically, the entire European Jewish community.

Very few Jews survived the storm of hatred and prejudice that swept across Europe and decimated six million souls.

The story of Avrum and his sister Lena is only one of many stories that have helped to build the substructure of faith and belief among survivors of the Holocaust that is so necessary to reconstruct their lives. Their story, and those of the precious few survivors, told in this book are stirring examples of the will, determination, and sheer luck needed to prevail against overwhelming odds.

The Precious Few is a work of fiction based on a thousand true stories.

1

AVRUM

JANUARY 1941 TO MARCH 1941

I am Avrum

My name is Avrum Bielinski. I am a survivor of the Holocaust. I'm 76 years old, and live in Cleveland, Ohio, a far cry from Poland where I was born and had planned to live my life.

I'm at a park with my 12-year-old grandson, Jacob, a creature of tireless energy and curiosity. We come here so he can play with his friends and find joy in the freedom of a worry-free environment. While he plays, I usually read a newspaper or a book, and take delight in watching him be his energetic self. Today, his friends are late, so we're sitting on a bench together, talking. Jacob just asked me a question that took me by surprise, since the subject had never come up before. He asked me why I had a number tattooed on my arm.

I never talked to Jacob about the tattoo, which I got when I was only slightly older than him, because the story is too sad and too hard to explain. Yet, he deserves to know. In fact, it's my duty to tell him, as well as others. I often speak to various groups to explain the history of the Jews in Europe during World War II. It's a tragic history that must never repeat itself.

I hesitate to tell Jacob, because he is so young. Still, he needs to know. Everyone needs to know and remember.

My Beginnings

I was born in 1926 in the small town of Leszno, Poland. Two and a half years later, my mother told me that I was going to have a brother or sister. Lena was born in 1928. When my mother told me that I now had a sister, I took that to mean that she was mine—my possession. I always went out of my way to look after and protect her. She followed me everywhere, like a little puppy. My mother and father always called her Leah, which mystified me. I couldn't understand why they did that. I would later learn that we each had a formal name and an affectionate name. "Leah" was Lena's affectionate name.

When I was old enough, my parents sent me to a school attended by Jewish children only, since in our town Jews all lived in the same area. My father was a tailor, so he did business outside of our neighborhood. He knew many Polish people, but we didn't socialize with them. Sometimes, I accompanied him when he delivered the clothes he had worked on and found it to be an exciting treat to meet his customers. The Jews in our little town seemed to get along with the gentile Polish residents and they also seemed to get along with us, but we didn't mix with them except for business. I asked my father about that once and he told me that most of the Poles got along with us just fine, but there were some who didn't like us.

I asked why and he said he'd tell me when I was older. I knew that meant the conversation was over but was sure that someday I would get an answer.

Our house was a happy one with wonderful Shabbos dinners. The dinners were very special, even though they happened weekly. They celebrated the sacred day of rest among Jews, from sundown on Friday to sundown on Saturday. It was a time of celebration and family—a true joy. Sometimes my grandparents would come to the dinner. They always spent a lot of time with Lena and me and I must admit that I loved being doted upon by them.

When I was small, my mother used to sing to me at bedtime while my father stood and watched. I enjoyed that immensely. When Lena came along, my mother sang to us both. She used to sing a song that she had made up just for us:

> "Little child, little child, go to sleep,
> Whatever you dream is yours to keep,
> So close your eyes and you will see,
> Sugar plums and a candy tree,
> Big white birds flying free,
> Hugs and kisses from Poppa and me."

I especially enjoyed sharing this special moment with my sister. Those were wonderful bedtimes and moments never to be forgotten.

Our Village

The inhabitants of Leszno were mostly Polish, with a few Ukrainians and a vibrant Jewish community of about 6,000. The Jews got along pretty well with the Poles, even though there were instances of antisemitism, but they did not get along with the Ukrainians. While the Jews did business with the gentile Poles, they didn't socialize with them.

Out in the village and in the marketplace, the Jews spoke Polish, but among themselves, they spoke Yiddish: a Germanic language that began with the German Jews and then spread across Europe as they fled Germany and settled across the continent. Jews from different European countries easily conversed with one another thanks to their shared ancestral language. A few could also speak a little Ukrainian.

My father was a tailor and had some Polish customers that he called his friends. Most of the surrounding villages and cities had robust Jewish populations. The Catholic Church was very strong in our area and on Sundays everything shut down. In this setting, the Jews prospered doing their business and attending their synagogues.

One Sunday, I asked my father why the Poles and Jews lived so differently.

"The Poles are Catholic, and we are not," he answered. "The Jews moved to Poland a few hundred years ago, while the Poles were already here. They think that we are like renters, and they are the landlords. Many Jews dress differently and that makes them stick out.

Poles look at our businesses and think we are rich. They think we group together and help each other out and scheme together to take advantage of the Polish gentiles. I believe they are jealous, a big reason why they dislike us. And the Catholic Church isn't of much help. They're not tolerant of other religions, especially ours. Even more of a problem is that some of the Poles think we are communists and loyal to Russia. That's not true, but that's what they are told and believe."

"Poppa, what is a pogrom?" I asked. I had heard two teachers in school talking in whispers and one said that word like it was a secret or a bad word.

"A pogrom is an ugly thing. It's the organized persecution of helpless people, in our case, against Jews. It often leads to massacre. Hoodlums try to hurt people and destroy property. They get into a rage and lose control. People take out their jealousies and frustrations, using the Jews as their targets. A pogrom is people losing their minds and venting their hate. It's a sickness of the ignorant. I hope we will never see one in Leszno."

"Me too, Poppa," I agreed. "I hope we can live in peace here."

Shabbos Dinner

Friday night was here. We honored the Sabbath with food and family. Mamma always made chicken and sometimes lokshen kugel, a wonderful baked noodle dish, and also challah, a traditional egg bread. The house smelled delicious. This Shabbos we were having my mother's parents over, my Bobba and Zeda, Yiddish for grandmother and grandfather. My father's brother, Uncle Nathan, and his family, as well as my mother's sister, Aunt Hannah and Uncle Daniel were also coming. The women were all bringing something delicious, and I would get to see many of my cousins. The women lit the Shabbos candles and the men followed by saying a prayer for wine and, of course, the hamotzi: a prayer over the bread. The meal was, as always, special.

After dinner, my cousins and I were told that we could go play. The women went about the usual business of cleaning up, and the men, instead of their usual gathering to chat and tell stories, decided to hold a meeting. Since most of my cousins were younger than me, I asked if I could stay with the men. They looked at one another quite seriously and gave their consent, but they told me that whatever was discussed could not be repeated outside the room. I was excited.

My father was the first one to speak. "I asked you all to be here at this wonderful family dinner so we can discuss the events that are happening around us. Wherever we Jews go, it seems that we are treated like second-class citizens. In spite of that, we thrive, but the better we do, the less our neighbors seem to understand and appreciate us. The less they like us. I know you are all aware of the horrible treatment our brethren are receiving in Germany, and I am concerned that perhaps the same thing could happen to us here in Poland. So I ask you, can it happen here, and if so, how do we protect our families?"

Uncle Nathan spoke next. "As you know, my business causes me to travel and one of my destinations has been Germany. I am not sure if I can go back there to conduct my business, nor do I want to. The Germans are under new laws, stealing all the Jewish property they can get their hands on. They're taking away the privileges from the Jews that all other German citizens enjoy."

Looks of concern and anger filled the eyes of the men as they glanced at one another.

"Last month, they evicted all Jews with Polish citizenship. The majority of them has been crammed into the village of Zbaszyn. There has been an escalation in acts against Jews. I cannot even imagine what could happen next."

Uncle Daniel spoke up. "Nathan, what should we do? Can we pick up and leave? Is that possible? I don't think the Poles will copy the Germans in their treatment of the Jews."

My father said, "As a tailor, I could pick up and leave, but what about my parents? Where could I even go? And how could I take along my family?"

The predicament prompted a long silence.

Daniel suggested, "I think it would be wise to consult the rabbi and others who may have some answers."

As a community, we are all faced with the same problem. We can't imagine what cruel things they could do to us, because our minds don't work that way. We're not in Germany. But we have to consider that perhaps this anti-Jewish disease could come to Poland."

My father rose and addressed the group. "It is a scary time. Let us seek advice, as Daniel suggested. But I feel we must not wait too long to come to some decisions on the protection of our families."

Everyone agreed and the meeting ended. I left with the barest clue that events were about to take place that would change my life as well as the lives of millions of Jews and oppressed peoples throughout the world.

Young Avrum

On September 1, 1939, Germany fabricated a political excuse to start a war with Poland. After World War I, the Treaty of Versailles punished Germany by awarding productive geographical areas to the victors of that war. This made Poland a beneficiary of Germany's loss. Hitler felt he could take over all of Poland quickly and efficiently, virtually overnight, and that other nations wouldn't wage war on them over that supposedly small move. He was right. He initiated the first blitzkrieg, the sudden application of overwhelming force on a concentrated target, which proved to be dramatically effective. The German war machine sent its airplanes and tanks and one and a half million soldiers to crush a weak and unprepared Polish army. It was no contest. The Poles took a severe beating, losing the conflict in a mere month. The Germans moved so fast that by the time the people in our village heard that we were at war, it was over. Poland had been defeated. For us, it was bad news after bad news—with worse news to come.

We had already heard horrible stories of what the Germans were doing to the Jewish population in their own country. It was hard to grasp the enormity of it. Some of the Jewish residents of our village had already packed up and moved east. Then, one day, the Germans rode into our village on motorcycles, tanks, and trucks. Soldiers appeared everywhere, taking over all authority in the village. They immediately imposed new laws on all residents: Poles, Ukrainians, and Jews.

The new laws for the Jews were suffocating and harsh. We had to wear a yellow Star of David patch on our jackets or other outerwear apparel. The Germans imposed a curfew on us and enforced a law that said that we must only walk on the roads and stay off the sidewalks. I heard my father talking about some tax contributions from all Jewish residents to be paid to the German authorities. As if that wasn't enough, they required the Jewish community to provide a free labor force every day to help the German cause. The hours were very long and the work difficult. The life we had known was painfully disrupted.

While all of this was going on, more Jews who had left their own villages and cities showed up, thinking conditions were better in Leszno, but they weren't. Food became scarce. The new laws prevented all Jews from going to school. A profoundly sad day came when the Germans burned down all our synagogues but one. Some Jews were taken into the forest and shot dead.

We lived in terror, which, we quickly learned, was the Nazis' favorite tool of persuasion. Our parents, as well as our elders, didn't know what to do. Germany's plans for the Jews in Leszno, as well as the larger Jewish population in Poland and Europe, became clearer and more frightening each day.

Protecting Lena

I could hear my parents whispering. They were talking about taking Lena away to save her life. My father told my mother, "We cannot wait any longer. We cannot ignore the stories and rumors we're hearing. The Germans are rounding up all the Jews and sending them away to work camps, or so they say. They're suffocating the Jews with all their rules. We wear a yellow Star of David now. We must walk in the streets. The sidewalks are too good for us, and if we don't obey, they kill us. Every right has been taken away."

Mother sighed, her face dark with concern.

Father went on. "In the village of Cybinka, they rounded up all the Jews and took away the older people in trucks. None of them have been seen again. I'm told that children are of no use to the Germans if they can't work. There's more, but I think we all agree that our time is limited. We must try to save our children, if we can. There's no good future for us. Avrum is old enough and big enough to work, but our dear Lena is just a child."

My mother broke into tears. "What will we do?"

"Sophie," he said, "tomorrow, I will take Lena to a man I know who has agreed to take her in. His children are grown-up and moved to Warsaw, so he and his wife said they can take care of her. I'll give him some money, which I have promised, and he and his wife will look after Lena for us."

"Morris, who is this man? How do you know you can trust him? They say that if you help a Jew you can be killed. Why would he risk it? You know the Poles have not always been our friends."

"My friend is Mr. Kwalski."

"The clothing merchant?"

"Yes, that's him. He's an honorable man."

"Yes, he seems that way. Still, are you sure?"

"Do we have a choice?" my father went on. "I'll explain this to Avrum now, and in the morning, I'll tell Lena as best as I can."

My father came into my room and saw the teary eyes I tried to hide. "Avrum, I know you were listening. I hope you understand that we have little choice."

"I know. Will we be able to see Lena again?"

"I do not know, but we must do our best to survive this nightmare. We must protect her as best we can. When the time comes, God willing, we will find her again. I don't know what is in store for us. These Nazis are madmen."

I stared off into space, gathering my thoughts, trying to imagine the unimaginable.

"Listen to me, Avrum. If we get separated, you from your mother and me, you know how to be a tailor. You're very good at it. And you're already a big enough boy to do whatever work you're asked to do. I hope we can be together, but I don't know what exactly is going to happen. If something were to happen, God forbid, to Mamma and me, then you must find your sister and look after her as best you can. Do you understand?"

"Yes Poppa, I'll do my best." I stared into his eyes, to show my conviction.

"Okay. We'll say our goodbyes in the morning. Goodnight, Avrum."

I nodded my head in agreement, unable to say goodnight.

Then, Poppa went outside for a moment to collect his thoughts before having his talk with Lena. This wasn't going to be easy.

When he came back inside, she was sitting quietly in Poppa's favorite chair, waiting for him, knowing something important was taking place. Lena was only ten years old, but very bright. Poppa hoped he could make sense to her. He didn't notice me sitting on the sofa. I needed to be there for my sister.

"Lena, I know you are aware of what is going on with the treatment of Jews by the Germans," Poppa began.

Lena nodded quietly.

"More of our Jewish friends are disappearing every day and families broken up. We need to find a safe place for you to hide until, hopefully, things get better. I have spoken to my friend, Mr. Kwalski, who has agreed to take you into his home and hide you until things improve."

Tears welled up in Lena's eyes. "Momma, Avrum, and I will do our best to stay out of the way of the Germans until we can get back together as a family."

Poppa reassured her. His heart broke, watching the tears spill down her cheeks.

"I know Poppa," she said in a shaky little voice. "But isn't there any way I can stay with all of you?"

"No, Lena. That's a risk we can't take."

The Next Day

The next day we all tearfully said our goodbyes and Poppa took Lena to the Kwalski's.

When he returned home, the atmosphere was tense. Momma was

quiet and Poppa didn't have much to say either. That evening, I heard them talking. He told her that things were very bad and went on to explain how the oppressive measures the Jews were enduring in Germany had been put in place in Poland, as feared. He railed on with information he had told her before, but needed to say again, as the weight and pressure of it occupied his every waking moment. He went on about how Germans had imposed new rules and laws that took away the liberties and freedoms that the Jews had once taken for granted. He said that he heard that some Jews were taken away as workers for the Germans. He wasn't sure where they went, but they have not been heard from since. German soldiers in uniform were now everywhere.

Momma stared at the floor and sighed, "How can they do this? I don't understand."

"They do what they want. They have the power," Poppa said. He went on to explain that his friends asked him to be part of the *Judenrat*, a group formed by the German command, made up of only Jews. Members of the *Judenrat* were called upon to control the Jews in our town. When the Germans needed things to be done or needed laborers, they went to the *Judenrat* to provide the workers. Poppa decided that he did not want to be part of it. He chose to stick closer to home and watch over Momma and me.

Normal business was constantly disrupted by the Germans and local police, who appeared to enjoy torturing the Jewish population. Buying food became a very difficult task. People were trading their personal belongings with farmers for food. One day, the Germans raided our synagogue and took all the books—even our Torahs—and threw them into a pile on the street. They made all the Jews stand and watch as they set everything on fire. We were terrified and even the Poles were shocked.

Then came the fateful day when all Jews were told to pack one bag per person and go to the village square. We were frantic at home. Before we left our house Poppa sat me down and said, "Avrum, no good can come from this. They say we are going to a work camp, but it's hard to believe anything they tell us, especially since we've heard so many contradicting stories. If we do go to a work camp and they ask you what you can do, remember to tell them you are a tailor, like me. If they want you to do anything else, tell them you can do whatever they want. I'll do my best to look after Momma. And remember, if anything should happen to Momma and me, you must live to find Lena."

Unable to speak, I nodded. Then, carrying our meager possessions, we made our way to the village square. Once we got there, the soldiers lined us up. German officers divided us into different groups. The elderly were loaded onto trucks. The scene was heart-wrenching. Families were crying and hugging one another—fearful and confused. Then the trucks drove off, leaving a wake of silence.

Our Polish neighbors watched with mixed emotions. In general, antisemitism was strong among the Polish people, who had been taught that the Jews were responsible for the death of Jesus. Yet, even if they wanted to help in some way, it would have been impossible. Many of the spectators looked on with tears in their eyes and terror on their faces, not knowing where this brutality would end. The Germans marched us to the train station where we were herded in groups to stand before cattle cars. If we had been treated like cattle, that would have been more humane.

The Train Ride

The Germans loaded us into the old box cars. The stench of animals and their emissions was soaked into the wood. They shouted obscene threats while cramming us together until there was no room to sit. They allotted one bucket per car for everyone to use as a toilet. The entire process couldn't have been uglier or more degrading. Standing among the herd, being pressed and smothered by everyone around me, I held onto Poppa's coat as we huddled, wedged into a corner. He had his arms around Momma. As frightening as the whole process felt, I became progressively angry and determined to survive this ordeal. Finally, they shut the door. It was even more suffocating now. This was just one of the many cattle cars that were joined together, loaded with Jews from other cities and villages.

Finally, the train started, and we were on our way to some unknown destination.

"Avrum, are you okay?" My father's voice broke through the sounds of human suffering.

I said I was. I could hear the pain and anguish of our neighbors, their whimpers and groans. Fear permeated the entire train. I felt awful for all these good citizens who were being swept along on this dark course, fearing the worst, yet having no idea what would happen. What was their fate? What was ours?

On the journey, many people died from lack of air, water, and food. Occasionally, someone would faint, slide to the floor and, all too often, die. From time to time, we were put on a sidetrack to let German troop trains pass.

It took two painfully long days to arrive at our destination, Dachau. The doors opened, and the light of day exploded in our faces. It was so bright, we could barely see. The German soldiers ordered us into different lines. Snarling guard dogs, straining at their leashes, intimidated us. I watched Momma and Poppa still clinging together as I was pushed into a group of younger people. They took away our single suitcase and gave it to some prisoners who were already there to start separating the contents into different piles. We were told to undress.

All the while, they beat us with whips. They prodded and pushed, and those who fell were kicked and beaten. We were totally unprepared for such cruelty. They took us to a shed where they shaved our heads and stuffed the hair into burlap bags. Then, they herded us off to a place where they tattooed numbers on our arms, turning us into branded animals. Finally, they disinfected us with a chlorine solution and gave us striped uniforms to wear. The eerie sameness of our appearance made us all look like a new species of animal.

2

LENA
MARCH 1941 TO MAY 1942

The Kwalskis

My father took me to Mr. and Mrs. Kwalski. He spoke with them for a minute and then hugged me goodbye.

"My dear Leah," he said, "you must do as these wonderful people ask you to do. Never forget who you are. We hope we will all be together again. We love you."

He hugged me one more time, then turned and was gone. That was over two months ago. Mr. Kwalski is very nice to me, but his wife is formal and cold and not easy to talk to. I was told to never go out. Mr. Kwalski says the Germans must never find out that I am here. If they find me, the family will be put to death for hiding a Jew. What have the Jews done to cause people to be killed for being nice to them?

Mr. Kwalski has built a little place for me to hide in if the Germans ever come to this house. He is terrified that a neighbor will find out I am here and tell the Germans. I feel guilty for putting them at risk. We're reminded of that risk on a daily basis. Yesterday, we heard motorcycles and I had to go into the hiding place.

At dinner, they talk about how the Jews are being rounded up, taken away, and seen no more. I want to ask questions, but I am afraid to. I have been given chores to do and I am thankful that I can help. There's no school for me. In fact, there's no school for any Jewish children. I read whatever books are in the house to keep my mind active.

Last week at dinner Mr. Kwalski told his wife that the Nazis, as he calls the Germans, burned down two synagogues. His wife is getting more frightened each day and the atmosphere is tense at times.

Last night, I overheard them discussing that maybe it would be a good idea to take me to a Catholic convent. Mr. Kwalski guessed that if I pretended to be a Christian, they'd certainly take me. Maybe I would have to convert and actually be a Catholic.

The Kwalskis are getting more frightened each day. I'm beginning to think about running away. I could certainly blend into the Germans' idea of the acceptable race: the Aryans. My hair is sandy-colored and I have hazel eyes. Who could tell that I was Jewish? But what would I do? How could I survive? I will have to think about it. Maybe I can get some useful ideas from Mr. Kwalski.

Hiding

The roar of the motorcycles was deafening. It mixed with the heavy sound of trucks and voices out on the street. Orders, barked in German, echoed back and forth, coming closer to us. Mr. Kwalski ran to me and said, "Lena, follow me. We are going to the hiding place, and you must be careful. You must be quiet. Not a sound. Nothing! Do you understand?"

He grabbed my hand, and we quickly ran to the bedroom. He pushed a heavy bookcase to one side, exposing a narrow space between two walls. I forced my way into the space. It was tight and cramped, but I had practiced hiding here before. Then he pushed the bookcase back in front of the secret spot, blocking nearly all of it from view. The smallest crack between two boards allowed me to peek out, but I knew no one would be able to see me.

In minutes, a pounding on the door announced the arrival of the military. Mr. Kwalski sat at the table, eating, as his wife answered the door. She found a German officer and two soldiers standing before her. "What is going on?" she asked, trying not to sound alarmed.

"We are looking for Jews," said the officer. "Who lives here?"

Mr. Kwalski had risen from the table and made his way to the door. "Just my wife and me," he said. "Our children moved to Warsaw to work."

"Well, a neighbor told us that they thought there was someone else living here. Stand aside, we will look for ourselves." They barged into the house.

"Please, don't break anything," Mr. Kwalski said. He put his arms around his wife, who was shaking.

The house wasn't very big, so the search was going fast. The soldiers opened closets and cabinets and carelessly poked at everything. The officer asked, "Who sleeps in this small bedroom?"

Mr. Kwalski said, "My children used to, but as I told you, they are in Warsaw."

He was interrupted by one of the soldiers, who announced that they found nothing.

"Good," the officer said. "Let's get on to the next house. We still have a lot of work to do." Then he turned to the couple and said, "Don't forget—anyone hiding or helping a Jew will be shot or hanged."

I was perspiring profusely in my small, tight space, concentrating on breathing lightly. I was afraid I would wet myself. The Germans marched out, slamming the door to make their point. I stayed in the same crouched position for a very long time, cramped and miserable. Eventually, the sounds of vehicles and soldiers faded. The Germans had finally vacated the area, leaving as abruptly as they came.

Mr. Kwalski took no chances and had me stay in the hiding space. The Germans were known to leave a search area and then sneak back suddenly to catch those who thought it was finally safe to come out of hiding. Their strategy had been remarkably successful.

After what felt like hours but were really only minutes, Mr. Kwalski moved the bookcase and helped me out. "Are you okay, child?"

I said I was and went to wash up.

Germans

I could hear Mr. and Mrs. Kwalski talking. They were frightened after the soldiers' intrusion into their home. The Germans used threats and bribes to tempt citizens to turn in Jews. Mrs. Kwalski said that she heard that the Germans are offering a pound of sugar for every Jew turned in.

Mr. Kwalski sighed. "How could such a reward be good enough to make a Pole turn in a fellow neighbor? It disgusts me. But what really bothers me the most is that one of our neighbors is watching us and willing to betray us. They know that to help a Jew is punishable by death."

After a moment's pause, Mrs. Kwalski said to her husband. "Jan, I am not only worried about us, but I am worried for the child as well. I hear her humming every night, a song that her mother taught her, and I can feel her pain. She is a quiet and nice girl, but I am afraid now that we shall all be discovered. I think that perhaps the time has come to take her to the convent. We could speak with Reverend Mother Karina Szymanski. I've spoken with her many times at church. I am sure we can trust her."

"I am confused about what should be done," he replied. "We are entrusted with a child's life. What would her parents say about her being thrusted into a Catholic environment, a child who is Jewish? Should we tell the Reverend Mother that she is Jewish? Would we be endangering the convent?"

She shook her head and stared at the floor, unable to answer.

"I don't know what to do," he went on. "We must think it through. What would Bielinski do with his daughter if we didn't take her?" After a long silence, he straightened up and spoke with a new conviction. "I know you are right. She can't stay here. We are all in danger. Avrum Bielinski gave me money to take care of Lena and I won't cheat him. I don't know if she'll need papers at her age. I'd better find out and see what can be done."

I realized the problems I was causing the Kwalskis and tears flooded my eyes. They had taken a chance by trying to save me from the Germans, as my father told me they would. I was in no position to make things different or better than they were. Should I run away? But where could I go? No, I would have to wait and do whatever the Kwalskis decided. My father trusted them and so must I.

Mother Superior

Karina Szymanski, the Mother Superior of the Convent of the Sisters of St. Nazareth, sat in her office behind closed doors and pondered on the turbulent events going on around her. She, with the help of 12 loyal nuns, was struggling to keep the convent open and viable to support the many children they had under their care.

The Germans had openly made their plans known about what they intended to do with the Jews, Gypsies, and anyone they considered to be in their way, even certain Polish politicians. Now the Nazis were also destroying the Polish Catholic church. Large numbers of priests were being taken to a place called Dachau, never to be heard from again. Convents and churches were being closed by Hitler's orders. The priests and nuns were taken away and killed, so she heard. Yet some of the convents were still open. Hers was one of them. She didn't know why, but she thanked God many times a day for being an exception to the rule. It seemed like every day someone showed up with a child who needed a safe home. She knew that many of the children were Jewish, but chose to ignore that fact, even though the risk was enormous.

Today, she had an appointment with Mr. Kwalski, a good Catholic who she knew had a child living in his house who was neither his own nor was family. She had a strong suspicion about what he wanted. Chances were good that the child was Jewish, posing a danger to her and the convent. She thought to herself, *I know we have a few Jewish girls already here, but I cannot hesitate to help a child, Jewish or not. I pledged to love Christ, who himself was a Jew and helped those in need. When I think of the Jews, I think that the Catholic Church has not done them any favors in the past. Indeed, they are people of the Bible. They have close families and seem to be a studious, God-fearing people who are dedicated to learning.*

A brisk knock on the door interrupted her thoughts. One of the nuns announced, "Reverend Mother Karina, Mr. Kwalski is here."

The Convent

I was sad to leave the Kwalskis. As Mr. Kwalski explained to me why I couldn't stay in their home, it was obvious how badly he felt. I could tell how difficult this decision was for them. He had somehow gotten me a set of false papers, in case I needed them. He took me to the convent, where we found our way to the Mother Superior's office. He told me to sit in the anteroom, which was adjacent to her office. From that position, I could watch the two of them talk through the large open door. The Mother Superior, an older woman who stood with a posture of assurance and confidence, offered him a chair. I watched and listened closely to their soft voices in serious conversation.

"How may I help you?" she asked.

"Ah, these are difficult times, Reverend Mother. There are so many lost lambs in this world."

"Yes, so true."

"I have encountered one of those lost lambs. She's barely a teenager and has no place to go. Her family is gone. We would take her, but..." he lowered his voice, "there are difficulties that are hard to explain."

"No need to explain," she said, her eyes full of understanding. "We are here to give aid and comfort to the needy and the lost. That is our mission and duty."

Mr. Kwalski wondered if he should go on, but Mother Superior read the dilemma on his face and continued. "We are blessed to be in a position to bring God's comfort to this child. I'll be happy to accept her."

His face relaxed for the first time since he entered the convent. He understood the unspoken message. They talked a bit longer, then he stood to leave.

They came out to the anteroom, both looking more relaxed than when they had entered. She was warm and comforting, yet exuded confidence and a no-nonsense attitude.

We spoke for a few minutes, then she turned me over to Sister Franceszka, a young, energetic nun with a wonderful smile. I was told that she would get me settled in. The Mother Superior whispered something in her ear. They both smiled knowingly and then turned to face me and Mr. Kwalski. The Mother Superior nodded to him. He, as if given a signal that things were in order, gave me a warm hug, smiled at the two nuns, and left, casting one last woeful glance over his shoulder at me as he disappeared through the main archway. Sister Franceszka motioned me to follow her.

As we walked to the dormitory, she explained that there were more like me—saying those words in a hushed tone—and that there were girls living here of all ages. The girls stared at me while I was shown where to sleep and put my things. I was given a regular schedule and realized that I had much to learn in order to blend into this gentile group . All the girls had jobs and responsibilities. There were gardens to maintain, sewing, cleaning, kitchen duty, and work brought to us from outside for which the convent was paid to help sustain its existence. There were also prayers to be said on a regular basis during the day and in the evening. They were difficult for me at first, but all the girls learned them. I resented them. My parents would be sick if they heard me saying Catholic prayers, spouting words and ideas foreign to me and my religion. However, if doing that would keep me alive, then that is what I had to do.

The nuns knew I was Jewish, and that they were taking a big chance to have me in their convent. The penalty was death but, for whatever reason, the Germans left the convent alone. The property had a wall around it with big gates that gave us a lot of privacy. I knew that there were other girls here who were Jewish, but I didn't know which ones. Some seemed Jewish to me in their looks and behavior, but I was careful to avoid the subject.

I quickly made some friends. Having other people my age around me was a big comfort. My best friend was Irena: a girl about a year and half older than me from a small village not far from my home. I didn't know much about her, but she was nice to me and I liked her.

One day, when we were alone, she asked me, "Are you Jewish?"

I didn't know what to answer. That was a dangerous thing to say in these times. "Who wants to know?" I asked.

"I know you are! I can tell," she gushed." Before I could answer, she said she was Jewish too.

I heaved a great sigh of relief. I had thought that she might be Jewish, but I didn't ask, in case I was wrong. From that moment on, we became very close. It was a great comfort to know that I was not alone. We thought that there were more Jewish girls in the convent, and we talked about who they might be, but we were careful not to disclose our secret. We told one another about our families and experiences. It was good to have a friend.

Irena's Secret

One evening, she surprised me when she confessed that Irena was not her real name. She said she took that name because that was the name on her false papers that her father managed to get for her. Her actual name was Natalia Lubinska, but she cautioned me to never use that name. She said that when her father brought her to the convent, the Mother Superior told him that she would do as much as she could for her, to ensure she could stay. It was an extremely big decision, because if the Germans found out that there were any Jewish girls in the convent, they would kill everyone. The Mother Superior spoke with all the sisters and confirmed that Irena could stay. Her father was vastly relieved, even though he was forced to leave her. He had heard about roundups of Jews and stories of them being taken away and disappearing. He did his best to make sure she was protected

Irena had three older brothers. When the Germans came, they all left, with the blessing of their father. The oldest brother, at 22 years old, went to Warsaw. The other two—ages 18 and 20—went to the forest to join the partisans. I had no idea what a partisan was, so I asked. She told me they were people of various backgrounds who wanted to fight the Germans. They formed fighting groups and camped out in the forest, where they lived off the land and whatever peasants would give them. I was in awe of the idea of Jews actually fighting the Germans.

I asked Irena if it bothered her that she was Jewish.

"Absolutely not! I am proud to be Jewish. I know some of the nuns would like to see me convert, but that won't happen. I miss my family and our wonderful Shabbos dinners. I miss my Jewish friends, and I miss celebrating our holidays. My father told me to stay Jewish no matter what. I hope you feel the same way, Lena."

I said that I did and asked Irena why the Germans were so against us.

"I'm not sure, but what I really don't understand is why so many Polish people hate Jews. They even say we killed Christ."

"How could we do that? We weren't even there," I said. "That was too long ago. Nobody Jewish I know killed anyone."

"I don't know," she said. "Thank God the nuns in this convent are brave and good people."

We nodded quietly and slipped into a moment of contemplation.

Irena broke the silence. "Do you think you'll ever see your family again?"

I stared into her eyes, looking for an answer. This was a hard thing to think about. We were all aware by now of what was going on outside the convent. We didn't know the details, but we knew the Germans were trying to kill the Jews, which is why we were hiding within these safe walls. We could not fathom why the Germans wanted to do this. In our town, the Jewish people hurt no one. We felt like we fit nicely into the community. We went about our business and kept to ourselves. We did business with the gentiles, the Poles, and Ukrainians who lived there, but we didn't socialize with them. We were better educated because we went to school, and to us, learning was important. The Poles went to school as well, but many dropped out to work. I told her that I didn't know if I would see my family again but could only hope that they would survive this terrible time.

Irena said, "You know, it's crazy that the Germans hate the Jews, and also the Poles, so I am told. And the Poles, it seems, don't care for the Jews either. Don't you think the Poles and the Jews should be on the same side against the Germans? You know, maybe we could recruit all the saints that the nuns tell us about. Then those saints could create some of the miracles the nuns say they can do. Things would be much better."

We laughed.

In a lighter mood now, she asked me why I was always humming. I was surprised. I didn't realize I was. With a sigh, I told her how my Momma sang to me every night at bedtime, a song called "Little Child". She asked if I could sing it for her. We were alone, so I agreed. I started to sing but choked up, and couldn't go on. She understood. We realized it was almost time for prayers, and we hurried off so we wouldn't be missed.

The Gestapo

Early one morning, we heard the bell ringing. This meant that the nuns were calling an important meeting for everyone. We immediately made our way to the chapel where they were waiting for us. We all filed in and sat down. Once we were settled, Mother Superior addressed us "Children, we are hearing stories of the Germans investigating convents and orphanages. They are looking for Jewish adults or children. I am telling you this because these Germans are very intimidating. As I am sure you know, to help a Jew means death. It is sad to think that helping another human being could result in the penalty of death. If they come here—and I pray they do not—then we must present your papers to them. The sisters will now show you your papers, so you are familiar with them. When you're finished going through them, please pass them back to the sisters for safe-keeping. I am sure that we have nothing to worry about. If you have questions, please ask any of the sisters. Let us pray now that the Germans never come."

After the meeting, Irena and I went to the garden.

"Lena, my papers are not very good," Irena said. "The Mother Superior looked at them and allowed me to stay, but I am terrified that the Germans will know that they are not official."

"What will you do?" I asked.

"I don't know. I think we'd better do what they ask us to do. Let us pray."

After the Mother Superior's concerned warning, we panicked at every sound, but luckily the Germans did not come. Then, one day we heard all kinds of vehicles out on the street. First, we heard the roar of motorcycles and then the clatter of trucks, and finally the sounds of soldiers and orders being shouted. Those sounds were all too familiar to me. Everyone was wide-eyed and frozen in place. The sisters ran to collect us and take us to the chapel. We heard a knocking, then a pounding on the gate. The Mother Superior and Sister Franceszka opened the door, finding themselves face-to-face with a German officer dressed in black and, behind him, several soldiers.

"What do you need?" Mother Superior calmly asked the officer.

"Madam, I am the Gestapo. I am asking for your cooperation. We are searching all convents, not just yours. We are looking for Jews. You know it is illegal to have them and help them. The penalty is death. Now I want to see all your girls, immediately. And make sure they bring their documents."

She had the sisters collect all the girls. We had each been given our papers and were lined up for inspection. I was terrified, held hostage by one frightening thought: *I am a Jewish girl with false papers.*

The Gestapo officer took each girl's documents, scrutinized them, then gave a long look into the face of each girl, trying to make her think that he knew the truth and could read it on her face. Then, content that the body language and facial expression appeared innocent, he moved on to the next girl. He took a step back from the girls. Looking very irritated, he turned to the Mother Superior and said, "Madam, we are one girl short."

"Yes," she said, "we have one girl who is sick and in the hospital."

He became very angry and demanded to see the girl. The only person missing was Irena. I didn't know what to do. The officer, along with four soldiers and Mother Superior, exited briskly and went to the hospital: a room with six beds and cabinets full of medicines and medical paraphernalia. They opened the door with a rush, as if expecting a hiding partisan. There, in bed, lay Irena, covered with ugly red marks over her face, arms, and legs.

Mother Superior spoke up. "We think she has scarlet fever."

The Gestapo officer gave Irena a hard look as he took a long step back, then turned on his heel and took three strong strides to the door. He stopped momentarily, turned to Mother Superior and said curtly, "We are done, madam. Things seem to be in order. And remember, do not take in any Jews." With a final intimidating glare at Irena, the officer wheeled around, ordered his men to join him, and quickly exited.

Mother Superior closed the door after them—a quiet little smirk on her usually serious face—and watched the soldiers stride away and disappear.

As fast as they came, they were gone. I had no idea what had happened. Later, Irena told me she had taken a needle and scratched herself so badly that it looked like she had scarlet fever. She thought it was funny, but I just shook my head. It had been a frightening experience, even though the outcome was good. I'll always remember the bravery of Mother Superior and the sisters.

After the German Visit

Everyone in the convent was stressed by the visit of the Gestapo. We had no idea how long it would be before they would come back.

Irena was especially nervous, and confided, "I can't do that scarlet fever thing again."

She asked me what I thought about leaving the convent. She suggested that maybe it wasn't as safe as we had thought it was. It was easy to see the concern on the faces of Mother Superior and the sisters. They were putting themselves at great risk by protecting us.

I missed my parents and my brother Avrum terribly. Where were they? Were they okay or had they been taken to one of the death camps we had been hearing about? Every day we heard terrible stories from people who delivered things and others who just came to visit. Most of the stories were about Jews, but also involved Poles and anybody who got in the way of the Germans.

Irena, frustrated, had not heard any news about her family—good or bad.

One night, after prayers, she said she had a question for me. We found a private place in the garden area, where she asked me again what I thought about leaving. I didn't know what to answer. Leave and go where? Maybe to a ghetto where there were other Jews? If we left the convent, how would we, two young Jewish girls, manage to avoid being noticed? We had papers, but would they hold up? Where else could we go and be safe? We knew that the ghetto was not a safe place.

Irena suggested that perhaps we could find her brothers in the forest. That stopped me. Leaving the convent was one thing, but trying to find her brothers somewhere in a forest sounded very difficult. Whether we found them or not, I was mostly a city girl and the thought of living in a forest sounded impossible to me. I told her about my concerns. I also added that the convent had looked out for us.

"Lena, we could be partisans. We could fight the Germans."

My knowledge of the partisans was limited, even though I had heard stories about what they did. I told her I would think it over.

That night, I lay in bed and tried to imagine what living away from the convent and its protection would be like. I tried to imagine living in a forest. Where did the partisans get their food? How did they stay warm during the winter? Would Momma and Poppa approve? And what about Avrum? Would he approve? I decided I would tell Irena that I needed a couple of days to decide. In truth, I was already leaning towards leaving the convent. I didn't think I could take another raid by the Germans.

Anna

Two days later, a new girl—Anna Polenska—was introduced to everyone. She was about the same age as Irena, which made her older than most of the girls in the convent, including me. Irena and I both noticed that she had a tough time with her prayers. She also kept to herself, which, of course, was not unusual for a new girl joining the convent. I asked Irena what she thought about Anna. I had my own thoughts, but Irena was older and had a lot more experience. I respected her opinion.

After prayers and dinner, we sat together and she said, "I am sure Anna is Jewish."

"Oh?" I answered. "What are you thinking?"

"We have to work in the garden tomorrow, and I think we can find the time to ask her."

I hoped she was Jewish. If some of the younger girls were Jewish, we were unaware, but it would be nice to have another Jewish girl our age living with us.

The next day was very hot, and we worked slowly in the convent garden. Lunch came, which gave us some time to eat, then rest and socialize. Irena and I were nervous. Suppose Anna was *not* Jewish. Would she tell the sisters we asked her that question?

"How could that hurt us?" Irena said. "The sisters are our friends."

"But would Anna expect the sisters to do something about it? And get suspicious if they didn't?"

"Hmm, look. You had a feeling about me when I first came here. You thought I was Jewish. So, you took a chance and asked. I trust your feelings."

"I really thought you were. And you are!" I smiled.

"I had the same feeling about you, but was too afraid to say anything," Irena went on. "I think it's worth taking the chance and ask. We can't both be wrong."

"I agree," I said. "Let's do it. You ask the question."

She took a deep breath, gave a half smile and said, "Okay, let's do it."

We found Anna sitting under the shade of a tree, eating an apple. Irena walked up to her and quietly said, "Excuse me, but my friend Lena and I want to ask you something."

"Yes?" she said.

"We think you're Jewish. Is that true?"

She looked at us but said nothing for a minute. Then she asked, "Why do you say that?"

Before Irena could answer, I blurted out, "We are Jewish. You can tell us."

Anna looked into our faces and said cautiously, "Yes, I am."

We all stood there for a moment, Irena and I smiling broadly. We were thrilled at being right. Anna brightened up and we hugged one another warmly. Since the next day would be a day of rest, we made plans to meet after morning prayers. Anna promised to tell us how she ended up here. She said she had plenty to say and couldn't wait to tell us. We could see that she really needed friends she could trust. We picked a time and as private a place as we could think of.

Anna's Story

The next day, we all met at a broken fountain behind the convent, a place rarely visited. Each of us was nervous, like we were committing some sort of a crime, but after a few moments we relaxed and asked Anna to tell us her story.

She cleared her throat, sighed, and began, "My real name is Hannah, Hannah Shaparowicz. I come from a family of five children. I have three brothers and a sister. My brothers are all grown up and have moved away. I know one was in the Polish army. I don't know about the other two. I have a baby sister. My family moved to the village of Libatchov, the name we used in Yiddish, but it's actually called Lubazow in Polish. We moved there so my parents could be close to family. We were originally from Krakow. I don't know exactly how many Jews lived in Libatchov, but I think maybe a little more than 1,500. Things were good for us there. We had some money from my father's business. He was a diamond merchant and traveled a little, but was home most of the time.

"Then the Germans came. They appointed a Polish police force to carry out their orders. They required all Jews to wear yellow Stars of David so they could be easily identified. Shortly after, Jewish schools were closed down. The Jewish community tried to figure out a way to get the Germans to open the schools back up.

"We put a strategy together and selected Jewish leaders to talk to the Germans, but it became immediately clear that they had a plan against the Jews. We were hearing ghastly stories of Jewish communities being rounded up and people disappearing. Then the Germans announced that they had designated the boundaries for a ghetto. One day, trucks full of Jewish people arrived and we were told that these people would live with us. Some of the people were from Oleszyce and other villages nearby.

"Our ghetto had twice the population it could support. There was an immediate shortage of food, water, and medicine. As the weeks passed, more families arrived and the situation in the ghetto got ugly. People were starving. There was sickness everywhere. They were surrounded by soldiers, who were just waiting for an excuse to show their power and authority.

"One day, the Germans told us to come out of the house and line up in the street. There were soldiers everywhere. An officer announced that the Germans needed workers. He told a large portion of the people to pack one bag and report back in one hour. It was crazy. People were crying and many families were split up. Some of the people tried to hide, but the German soldiers and Polish police looked in every house. They took half the ghetto away. My family wasn't picked. That night, my father left our house when it was dark and snuck back in after midnight. The next morning, both he and my mother told me I must leave.

"My little sister was too young to go, but my father had worked out a deal with a Polish man he knew to take me to a convent. He had paid the man with diamonds. My father knew the man for many years and trusted him.

"I was crushed to have to leave my family, but my father said we must survive as best we can. Hopefully, we will all survive, but who knows? My mother sewed a few diamonds into a piece of my clothing, and we all went to bed. The next morning, another large group of Jewish people from other villages arrived, and every house received a load of them. The limited supplies we had disappeared in a hurry. We had close to 20 people in our house where only a few lived before. The next night, when it was dark, my father took me to a Polish part of town to a Mr. Wosniecki. My father and I hugged. I couldn't imagine never seeing him again. And now, I'm here with you two, two more Jews, hiding and trying to survive."

Irena and I gave Anna a big hug and told her how we appreciated her story and that she could count on us to be good friends.

Lena's Thoughts

That night, I couldn't stop my mind from thinking as I lay in my bed and tried to understand the things Anna had told us. It's no wonder my father and mother had tried to spare me such a fate. What have the Jews done that so much pain should be put upon them? I'm young, but I understand family and how they love and support each other. I'm a teenager now, but I feel that I'll never know the life of a teenager. This convent protects me, but there is no love as great as the love of family.

I miss Shabbos dinners. Will I ever light candles again with my mother? Will my father ever give Momma and Avrum and me a piece of challah bread again? There is no Bobba and no Zeda to hold me and tell stories. Sadly, I am not alone in my suffering. The ghetto and other Jews also suffer. I am helpless and can't do anything for them. My friends, my relatives and my teachers are disappearing, maybe even dying.

When I see Irena this morning, I'll tell her that I think we should join the partisans. Why not? Even young girls can fight the Nazis. Someone will have to show me what to do, but I'll do what I am told. I must do something. We all must fight back.

To the Forest

The wind felt fresh on my face. Irena, Anna, and I were in the back of a farmer's cart on our way to the Parczew forest. We had gone to Mother Superior and told her what we hoped to do. She warned us of all the things she thought could happen to us, but after a long discussion, she gave in. We had tears in our eyes because the entire convent had risked their lives to protect us. If we had been discovered, they would all have been put to death.

Mother Superior had made an arrangement with a farmer who provided vegetables for the convent to take us to the forest, which was actually beyond his farm. He was happy to get us there. He welcomed having the opportunity to do something against the Germans.

Now, bouncing around in the noisy wooden cart, we were on our way to the Parczew forest, where Irena was positive that she could locate her brothers. Anna and I weren't so sure it would be as easy as she believed, but we were excited to leave the convent and do our part.

We stopped that night at the farmer's place, where we were rewarded with a wonderful dinner cooked by his wife. I wondered if perhaps this would be our last hot meal for a while. Then, with our tummies full and our minds even fuller, we were shown to a large room, where the three of would share a single straw-filled mattress.

The next morning, we got an early start and, after a tedious ride in the rickety cart, we arrived at Parczew forest. The farmer's wife had packed us some food, for which we were very grateful. The farmer told us to take the path in front of us into the forest and the partisans would find us. We all gave him a hug and he departed. We didn't know what lay ahead of us in the forest, but we welcomed the adventure, the opportunity to finally take some action.

Standing on the outskirts, we marveled at the sheer size of the tree-filled land before us. It was ominously large and beautiful—inviting and foreboding at the same time. I thought about how we were just three young girls on our way to who knows where and who knows what.

I heard Irena's voice and looked up.

"You're humming your song again."

Of course I was. I always did when I got nervous. I sang in what was almost a whisper:

> "Little child, little child, go to sleep,
> Whatever you dream is yours to keep."

Irena smiled at Anna and me and pointed to the path the farmer had told us to take. "Let's go."

Walking in the forest was an awesome experience. It had its own sounds and its own smell. The path under our feet felt soft from years of fallen, decaying leaves. We were very alert now, watching for signs of human life, but there were none to be seen. We stopped for lunch in a small clearing surrounded by a thickly wooded area. Although we were tired from walking we weren't discouraged in the least. We were three teenage girls banded together by the common goal of finding our way to the partisans and to survive. It helped take the edge off our nerves that Irena was vaguely familiar with this part of the forest, since her family had lived in the area. We stopped to have a lunch of bread and cheese, all the time wondering if there were really Partisans looking for three Jewish teenagers. When we finished eating, we continued on, hoping someone would truly come out of the trees to welcome us.

The Partisans

I wasn't sure if Irena really knew where we were going, but I was reluctant to say so. Minutes turned into hours. We had stopped our chatting and just plodded on. Then, to our surprise, five raggedy figures emerged from the trees, surrounding us without saying anything. We abruptly stopped, our hearts pounding at the sight of them. They were young men, each with some kind of gun. The tallest of the group stepped forward and scrutinized us. Then, with a bellow of surprise, he shouted out, "Natalia! Is it my sister Natalia?"

Irena ran to him, almost knocking him over, and shouted, "Schmuel! Schmuel!"

Oh my! It was her brother! The person we were looking for had found *us*. We breathed a huge sigh of relief, glad to have stumbled upon comfort and security in the form of the five ragged figures before us.

Schmuel asked, "Natalia, what are you doing here?"

She lowered her voice to a confidential tone, "You must call me Irena. That's my new name, the name on my papers. You must never use Natalia."

"Okay, okay," he laughed. "I don't need to understand. I'm just so happy to see you... uhm... Irena."

She smiled at her handsome brother and said proudly, "We have come to join you. My friends and I want to fight the Germans."

"Did you bring guns?"

"No."

"Well," exclaimed Schmuel, "let's not talk about it here. Tell us who your friends are and we will go to our camp where we can talk about what we can do with the three of you. You know Irena, our brother Meir is here with us. He'll be delighted to see you."

Irena was overjoyed to find another brother.

The three of us followed the five partisans deeper into the forest. No one spoke. We walked at a brisk pace, with Irena by the side of her brother, Anna and I following. We looked forward to being introduced to Schmuel's companions. They were young and had patchy beards. Two walked in front of us and two walked behind. They were always on the alert, eyes darting from side to side to make sure we were safe from the Germans and unfriendly Polish peasants.

The forest was beautiful, thick with tall trees and heavy green underbrush. The sounds of birds singing all around made us feel welcome. We came to a lake that looked unreal, as though an artist had painted it. I had no idea how the boys knew where they were going, but they moved so swiftly that there must have been a purpose to their pace. I was getting tired but said nothing and neither did the other girls. Finally, we came to a place hidden in the trees where we found a large number of people.

Two young men, maybe 18 to 22 years old, came forward and greeted Schmuel. "What have we here?" one wanted to know.

"We shall see," Schmuel answered.

There were several other partisans, including women and a few children, standing around, watching. It was clear that Schmuel was one of the leaders.

A tall, spectacled man with a well-groomed beard stepped out from the group of Partisans and addressed Schmuel. "Well now, what have we here?"

"Sol, this is my sister, Irena, and her two friends, Lena and Anna," Schmuel announced. "They've come to help us."

"Oh?" Sol grinned, a twinkle dancing in his eye. He had been a schoolteacher, a huge bear of a man with a gentle and caring nature that never diminished during this bitter war. The conflict did, however, bring out the bear in him. "What can they do?" he asked.

Irena stepped forward. "I can do whatever I am asked to do," she said, "and so can my friends."

"Well, what *can* you do?" Sol asked, with a challenging smirk.

Anna said, "I can cook. And I know how to do carpentry, if that is what's needed. I can clean and fix rifles. I can fight too."

There was a moment of silence, and everyone turned to me.

"And you, Lena, what can you do?" asked Sol with doubt in his voice.

I was nervous but I spoke up in a loud voice. "My father was a tailor. I can sew, repair, and make clothes. I can also cook, and I will fight Germans."

Schmuel stepped forward and said, "Girls, you will be given duties and there will be people to show you what to do. We are all Jews here. We must all look out for each other. Pay attention to what you're told. Our lives depend on being aware of what is happening around us. Now, if I could have a moment, I must find Meir so he can see our little sister."

Schmuel and Irena walked off while Anna and I met some of the people we would be living and fighting with in the months to come. I wondered what Momma and Poppa and Avrum would think of me now. I was at peace, being in a place where I didn't have to hide my identity. I was with other Jews. I looked forward to doing my part. In happiness, I hummed to myself.

The Partisan Camp

Each one of us was given different duties. I was to help with the cooking and the sewing, if necessary. If there was more for me to do, then I would be told. We were shown where to sleep, which was basically a large hole in the ground, a sort of covered den. There were approximately 40 to 50 partisans in our group. Most were young men. It was kind of like living in a fairy tale: so many handsome young men, so many people of diverse backgrounds gathered together for a righteous common cause, feeling secure and protected, feeling supported and useful.

I saw Schmuel frequently since he often came to see Irena. I really liked him. He was direct and unassuming. I asked him a lot of questions and he was very patient answering them. We learned from him that everyone had lice, and soon after we had them, too. It was the end of summer and droves of mosquitoes plagued us as well. Both kinds of insects were a real health hazard. We did our very best to stay as clean as possible.

One evening, Schmuel came to our sleeping area. Irena and Anna had just left to go somewhere, so he sat down with me and asked how I was doing. I said I was doing quite well. Then I asked, "Why are there only Jews in our group?"

He looked at me with a quiet anger on his face. "The Poles don't like us. Their antisemitism is worse than their hate for the Germans. There are Polish partisans, but it is rare to find a Jew in one of their units. Further east, there are Russian partisans, as well as Ukrainian and Latvian. The Russians help most of those groups with food and supplies. We're not so lucky. We have to scrounge for our own food, guns and bullets. Some of the Polish peasants help us, and we're grateful, but many do not. So, sometimes we have to take what we need, which makes for unfriendly peasants who also become our enemy. Some peasants report us to the Germans or to the Polish authorities who come after us. That's why it is difficult to have a permanent base. We have to be on the alert and ready to move at a moment's notice."

Questions flooded into my mind. "How did these people find you and your brother? How did you find them? Where did they come from? How did they get here?"

"We are a diverse group. Some people came from big cities and small villages, others from the ghettos. There are also people here who have escaped the death camps. Almost all have lost relatives and friends, some have lost whole families. Our group is made up of survivors and fighters. They know they are Jews because the world won't let them forget it. We help each other, and we understand that we need each other. We also understand that anything we can do to disrupt the Nazis is a step in the right direction."

"Are we the largest partisan group?"

"Oh no, there are bigger groups. There are many, some Jewish and some gentile. They are not only in our forest, but also in other forests throughout Poland, Latvia, Lithuania, Russia, Yugoslavia, and throughout Europe—all of them actually fighting the Germans and Italians."

"Can I go on a raid?" I asked. "Can I help?"

"Well," he said, stalling for time to find the right answer, "I will think about it. I'll discuss it with Sol and Zygmund. This is an important decision and I want to have their thoughts on it." He stood up and smiled. "It's time to sleep now. We will talk some more soon." Then he was gone.

I was excited. So much to think about! I hoped that I could fall asleep. I was so charged up about the possibilities ahead of us, my mind was dancing. But the constant activities in the camp put a lot of pressure on the mind and body and left us exhausted by the end of day. So, falling asleep wasn't a problem, after all.

3

MOLLIE
MAY 1942 TO APRIL 1943

Mollie

The clickety-clack of the train's wheels on the track was hypnotizing. I was part of a mob, crammed body to body in a cattle car with my mother, father, brother Nathan, sister Ruth, and countless others. There was absolutely no room to sit. We were hungry, thirsty, and scared. My father watched a boy tearing at the barbed wire covering a small window in the upper corner of the boxcar. He managed to remove the wire and immediately the younger people pushed to squeeze through the opening and jump from the window.

My father grabbed Nathan, Ruth, and me and shouted to us. "Run, run! It's your chance to stay alive. I'll stay with Momma, and we will try to find you later."

I think he knew that probably wouldn't happen. Older people helped to lift my sister, my brother, and then me to the window. We jumped, first Ruth, then Nathan, and after a last furtive look at Momma and Poppa, me.

I landed on a grassy slope and tumbled head over heels down the grade. I landed heavily on my leg, which hurt from the awkward landing. The Germans were shooting at us from the top of the rail cars. I lay on the slope and didn't move, hoping I would not be seen.

The sound of firing guns faded, then stopped, as the train disappeared out of sight. I saw a few young people running away and knew I needed to do the same. I tried to stand up, but my leg wouldn't hold my weight. I needed to move and frantically scanned the area around me for any kind of help. I saw a heavy stick lying on the ground and picked it up to support myself. It worked really well, and I started hobbling along the tracks to find my sister and brother.

I found Ruth first and then Nathan. The Germans had killed them both. This couldn't be real! My eyes filled with tears and grief consumed me, but there was nothing I could do. I was alone and had to move through the pain and anguish to a safer place. I clenched my teeth in determination and headed away from the tracks before another train with armed German soldiers on came along. My head was filled with fog and I couldn't think, but I knew I needed to find a place to hide and figure out what to do next. Though I could hardly walk, I managed to get away from the train tracks and sat down to rest.

A voice came out of nowhere, startling me. "Little girl, hello!" the voice yelled in Polish. I jumped, my heart pounding. "Are you hurt?"

I hesitated, and then slowly looked up to see the sun-parched face of a tall, thin farmer looking at me from about ten meters away. I answered that I was hurt.

In a soft, caring voice, he told me to stay where I was and that he'd be right back. When he turned and left, I was sure he was going to get the Germans, but what could I do? My ankle was swollen and throbbing with pain. After about 20 minutes I saw him coming back alone, leading a horse and a cart. I was relieved.

"Little girl, I'm back. Here is a piece of bread and some milk."

I was starved and saw only kindness in the farmer's face. I thanked him and devoured the bread and milk.

"I'm going to put you in the cart and take you home with me. I live close by with my wife. Some of our children have gone to the city, others joined the army. You are a Jew, right?"

I remained motionless, not sure what to say or do.

"Don't worry. That's all right with us. You can help Momma and me with chores on the farm. What is your name?"

"Mollie." It was too much effort to lie.

"My name is Janusz, but you should call me Poppa Jan. Come now, we will go to my farm. You will meet Momma Zofia and feel much better."

With muscular arms from a lifetime of farming, Poppa Jan lifted me up and put me on the straw-filled cart. He covered me with a blanket and lay straw on top of it so no one would guess there was a person in the cart. As soon as we started moving, I fainted into a deep sleep, exhausted from the chaos of the day.

On the Farm

Strong arms lifted me out of the back of the cart and helped me into a modest, but immaculately clean farmhouse. Farmer Jan introduced me to his wife, Zofia—an abundant woman with even more abundant warmth. She looked past my dirty clothes, the straw in my hair, and my exhausted demeanor, and smiled as she took my hand. "Child, I am glad you are here with us."

She told me that they would tell their neighbors that I was a distant relative who had come to help them in these troubled times.

"What is your name?" she asked.

"Mollie."

"Mollie," she said warmly, addressing me as if I were already a member of the family. "We will show you what to do. If you have any questions, ask either Poppa Jan or me. Now, let us fix your ankle and get you something to eat. After that you can rest."

Poppa Jan, Zofia, and their two farmhands helped me find my place on the farm. I learned how to milk cows, make butter, and help with making cheese. They even taught me—God forbid—how to feed the pigs! I spit three times just thinking about that. What would my family and my ancestors think about such a thing? A nice Jewish girl feeding pigs, but I was not in a position to complain. They gave me books to read, which really helped to fill my evenings and bring me beautiful dreams.

I was so thankful to be on a farm, away from the Germans and the horrible mess they'd made of everything. Poppa Jan worked very hard, and I did my best to be of help with anything he asked me to do. The other two workers felt like part of the family. One was an old man named Jerzy, who I never saw without his pipe. I could tell where he'd been during the day by the sweet smell of tobacco that lingered in the air for some time.

The other farmhand was a Polish girl named Catherine. She was a big girl, very strong and positive about everything she thought and did. Her parents had been killed in a German reprisal for what were considered to be acts of disobedience. Catherine was good natured and worked hard.

The care required to grow a variety of crops and raise farm animals kept us all busy. We grew potatoes, corn, wheat, and oats, as well as vegetables for ourselves. We also had cows for milk, from which we made butter and cheese. In addition, we raised beef cattle, poultry, and some pigs. Our nearest neighbor grew a great deal of sugar beets and a variety of fruit. Though I felt comfortable and safe, thoughts of family followed me like ghosts, leaving a trail of sadness. I tossed and turned many nights, hopelessly trying to sleep, but images of my family kept me awake. When I finally slept, the images persisted.

The days were long, but I was warm and well fed. I was usually relaxed, except for when we had visitors. I was afraid they might discover that I was Jewish. Then my farm family would be in trouble. Thank God that never happened. I became more comfortable with each passing day.

After about four months, Poppa Jan took me to the village marketplace to help him sell the produce we grew. I was nervous at first, but I became more comfortable with each visit. From time to time, German soldiers passed our stand to buy some produce. Whenever that happened, I found something to do, like washing vegetables or cutting off stems, and let Poppa Jan take care of the soldiers. On those days, I was always relieved when we closed our stand and went home.

Meeting the Partisans

After I had been on the farm for about nine months, Poppa Jan called me aside. "I have something to tell you. At the end of the week, we will have visitors. They'll be with us for about half a day. They are partisans, and we are going to supply them with whatever food we can spare and some clothing we've collected. This partisan group is Jewish. I have known them for a long time. They fight the Nazis, and we must help them when we can. I am telling you all this because we must get them loaded with supplies and away from here as fast as we can. Although I trust my neighbors, it is important that they do not know what we are doing. Do you understand?"

"Yes, Poppa Jan," I said. "I will do my best."

At the end of the week, early one morning, I saw a group of young people in carts coming down the road to the farmhouse. When they stopped in front, Poppa Jan went out to meet them with great enthusiasm. He and the leader of the group exchanged heartfelt greetings and embraced warmly, genuinely happy to see one another. Of the eight partisans, three were young girls about my age, all dressed in shabby clothes.

Poppa assigned me to work with a girl named Lena. We smiled at each other and went to work immediately. We enjoyed talking with one another as we brought food to the carts. I learned that Lena was slightly younger than me, but that didn't matter. Finally spending time with someone young was pure joy. I loved working with her. She told me that she didn't know where her family was either but thought about them all the time.

While we were loading things into one of the carts, we stopped for an instant and she asked me, "Mollie, are you Jewish?"

I was surprised and stunned by the question. I didn't know what to answer. Then I thought, *These are partisans fighting the Germans. There's nothing to fear here,* so I said, "Yes, I am." I was actually relieved to say it out loud. I felt like a Jew again, if only for a minute.

When we were done, we said our goodbyes and Lena and I hugged each other tightly. The feeling of kinship and warmth was as comforting as a Shabbos meal. We both hoped aloud that someday we would see one another again.

Later that night, as I lay in bed, I felt a comforting wave of emotion when thinking about the new, and wonderful friend I had just made.

4

AVRUM
MARCH 1943 TO SEPTEMBER 1943

Day after Day

Life in a concentration camp wasn't a life at all. People were dying every day from sadistic treatment, starvation, overwork, sickness, or a combination of those cruelties. We got up early every morning and stood like statues at roll call. Those roll calls and the counting of inmates seemed endless. Then we worked long days at whatever jobs we were assigned. When working in a quarry, I couldn't understand what we were trying to accomplish. We used picks and hammers to break up large rocks into smaller rocks, then smaller rocks to tinier rocks. We piled the rocks in mounds according to size. At some point, the rocks were loaded into trucks and hauled away. To where? For what?

As the weeks went by, it became more and more evident that the Germans had a dual purpose for us. On the one hand, they needed us to do the everyday work to maintain a camp like ours—like cleaning, sewing, carpentry, cooking, and so on. On the other hand, they were intent on eliminating Jews from the face of the earth by starving them, sending them to the gas chamber, or just killing them with their cruelty. According to their way of thinking, we were useful alive and even more useful dead. In a moment of dark humor I thought to myself, *At least Jews aren't useless.* I was told that while each camp was different, the treatment of Jews remained despicably constant and predictable.

There were inmates among us who were very skilled in various professions. These workers were used for various specialized needs. We provided the Germans with a range of specialists, including doctors, dentists, jewelers, carpenters, tailors, cooks, and more.

The Germans kept us so busy that at the end of the day we were too exhausted to socialize or develop friendships. Yet, the need to share our pain, fears and experiences with one another drove us to find kindred spirits. One day I met an inmate named Yankel. He was two years older than me. We tried to stay close to each other when we could.

I told Yankel that I intended to survive this ordeal so I could find my sister. He told me he also had two sisters and a little brother, but he had no idea where they were. He was with his parents and siblings when they were picked up by German soldiers. As he told me his story, I could see the pain on his face, but also a determination in his body language that said he would not allow himself to be crushed by the Germans.

Thoughts of escape ran through our minds daily, but we were terrified by how risky that would be. Then something happened that painted a very clear picture.

We were standing at roll call in the bitter cold one morning when we heard a commotion. All heads turned, and we saw three bedraggled prisoners being herded our way by a group of German guards and their vicious dogs. They were being pushed and prodded constantly as they stumbled forward with their heads down, trying not to fall. Finally, they were brought to a halt right in front of us. From the headquarters building, an SS officer and his personal guards strode to where we were standing and faced our group. After a moment, the officer announced to us that these prisoners had been caught while trying to escape. Talking through a megaphone, he said, "I have told you there would be punishment if anyone tried to escape. These three prisoners will be hanged. We will also pick out six more prisoners to be hanged as further punishment for disobeying camp rules." With that, the head guard walked over to where I stood and pointed his finger at specific men around me. I cringed as each finger found a target. I was glad it wasn't me, but devastated it was a fellow prisoner.

He called out, "You! And you! And you! And you!" And so on.

One of the men he had picked protested loudly. "Why me? I didn't do anything." His voice broke with emotion. "You can't do this! It's not right!"

Without hesitation, the SS officer took out his pistol and shot the man dead.

We were stunned, frozen in place.

He announced to the guards, "Pick out two more!"

We stood helpless, our minds trying to shut out the brutality of the scene before us.

Then the hanging took place, with typical cold German efficiency. Mentally I said Kaddish, the memorial prayer of respect for those who had died.

The *Kapo*

Every camp had a *Kapo*, a prisoner who acted as a foreman. The job involved giving us our work assignments and keeping us in order. Our *Kapo* was a man called Friedman. He was big, a beast, as most of the *Kapos* were. He seemed to enjoy hitting and kicking inmates. I did my best to avoid being wherever he was.

Our work details were a mixed assortment of inmates who were undernourished and slowly starving or newer workers who had more energy. The ages ranged from 16 to 60. The older and weaker inmates suffered from the wrath of Friedman, who never seemed to miss a chance to torment them with perverse pleasure. The days were always long, and it was not unusual for some workers to die on the job.

One extremely cold day, while working in the muddy forest just off a dirt road, two motorcycles came by with German soldiers on their way to who-knows-where. We had to get out of their way or be run over. Friedman slipped as he turned to watch the riders, causing his cap to fly off and into the road, where one of the motorcycles ran over it. He became livid as the soldiers disappeared and started to flail at anyone who was close by. He stopped for a moment and picked up his destroyed hat. Then he looked to see who else he could hurt to soothe the pain of him losing his cap.

Yankel shouted, "We can fix it! We can fix it!"

Friedman stopped and looked in his direction. I thought Yankel had made a horrid mistake to address Friedman directly.

"Who said that?" the angry *Kapo* growled.

Yankel repeated, "We can fix it."

Everyone froze in place, expecting a terrible scene.

Friedman strode up to my friend, his face still red with anger.

I feared for Yankel's life.

"How can this be fixed?" The *Kapo* asked, his face only inches away from Yankel's.

"Avrum can fix it," Yankel said, his enthusiasm overriding his fear. "He is a tailor."

Just then, two of the German guards asked what was going on and we immediately resumed work.

I had no idea what kind of position Yankel had put me in. His interference with Friedman had probably stopped him from beating us, but what now?

On the way back to the barracks, I whispered to him, "What have you done?"

"You can do it, Avrum. You can fix his hat."

We kept on walking. Later, after the evening roll call, we stood waiting to be given permission to line up for dinner and eat. To my surprise, Friedman came up to me and blocked my path to the food pots. He leaned into my face. "Are you really a tailor?" he asked.

When I said I was, he studied me closely and narrowed his eyes. "Can you really fix my cap?"

"I can," I said in a hoarse voice, and cleared my throat. "I will need a needle, some thread, and a place to work."

"How long will it take?"

"I am not sure. Maybe two days."

He straightened up and looked into the distance, as if trying to think of a truly creative punishment, while I stood and waited for his answer, hoping he would not find one. His eyes met mine again. "Maybe you will have to do it at night," he said.

"If I have to do it at night, it will take longer, but I can do it. I can fix it for you."

Friedman studied my face another long minute, then turned and left.

The next day, after work detail, he came to me, reached into his pocket, and held his clenched fist out to me. He opened his hand and offered me a needle, some thread, and a small scissors.

In a surprisingly soft tone, he said, "I will need the needle and scissors back. Go as fast as you can." Then, to my surprise, he handed me a piece of bread and left.

It had been some time since I had been given a job and told what it was for and why I was doing it. I felt myself relax and enjoyed a rush of pleasure from doing something constructive. I felt like a person who had value again. There was also a subtle change in Friedman's demeanor. This was only a temporary thing, but in this sea of evil and twisted events, this was a bright and fulfilling moment for me. I whispered to myself, "Thanks Yankel, for speaking up."

We are the Jews

One night, somehow, Yankel and I had a little time together. I asked him where he was from and how he got here. He told me he was from a small village in Poland, where he lived with his family. While he was away at a Zionist meeting, the Germans showed up in his neighborhood, rounding up Jews. He tried to get home to be with his family, but there were too many soldiers. He managed to get within eyesight of his home, where he saw his mother, father, two sisters and little brother being taken away. He thought he could get to his family, but soon realized that was impossible. As a lone, unarmed civilian, there was nothing he could do. He felt helpless as he watched most of the older people being led in different directions. Anyone who did not obey the Germans' orders was immediately shot. That night was filled with terror. All the Jews were taken to the rail yards where cattle cars were waiting for them.

Yankel and a few of his friends left the village and made their way to the Lodz Ghetto, where they could live with other Jews. The ghetto was inhumanely overcrowded, with residents so sick and starving, they could be of no use in a fight. He and his friends left with the idea of finding a partisan group and asking them to help fight these Germans. They had no food, so they stopped at a Polish farmhouse. The farmer told them he would feed them, but they could not stay, because it would mean death to him and his family if the young men were caught there. They thanked him and left, but a Polish peasant saw them walking away and turned them in for a bag of sugar. Yankel and his friends were taken to an internment camp and put to work.

As I watched him tell his story, I could see that he was getting progressively worked up. He said that he watched inmates die from disease and starvation only to be replaced by new inmates. Some of the inmates had better jobs and better food than others. He wondered why that was the case. Then, at the end of one day, when he and two other inmates labored on a work detail in the forest, they saw an opportunity to take advantage of the guards' sloppy vigilance. They managed to sneak away and escaped. The Germans searched and found them the next day and brought them back to camp, where they were whipped in front of everyone. The Germans decided to transfer him and some other prisoners to our camp.

Yankel told me that this whole experience had made him decide to be a better Jew. He would not let the Nazis take his Jewishness away from him. "I will live. I will survive and tell the world what has happened here. There are already rumors that the Germans are losing." Then he told me that something had been bothering him for a while, something he didn't understand. "You know, I see a German do horrible, vicious things, but this same German wears a cross around his neck. What a contradiction!"

"Yes, it makes no sense," I agreed. "They wear the cross as if it's only a trinket or jewelry. Not a conviction to do God's work. They're hypocrites. That's another reason I believe we will survive. We carry our belief in our hearts and minds. We believe in God and humanity, and in one another. Even if we are separated, we must find each other. I must live to find my sister no matter what."

We nodded at each other and fell asleep.

The Tailor

A week passed, each day mirroring the day before. Friedman was his usual intimidating self but seemed to avoid Yankel and me—a real blessing. I was skin and bones and not feeling well at all. It worried me. Then, on a cold, dreary morning roll call, Friedman and a German soldier stepped in front of us all and told me to come forward. Yankel's eyes widened as he glanced at me. I stepped out.

"Follow the soldier," Friedman said.

I did as I was told, with no idea where I was going or what was going to happen. The soldier took me to the hospital. I felt anxious and confused, with no idea what was going on. The nurses had been expecting me and told me to undress and take a shower. I was happy to do so. A civilized shower was only a thing of dreams here, not a reality. Immediately after the shower, the doctor came in. He carefully examined me and gave some orders to the nurses. I was frightened that I was going to be the subject of an experiment, but still asked no questions. One nurse gave me new clothing, which was starched and folded, and then she took me to a bed. She took my blood pressure and performed other tests, then brought me some food. I was ecstatic.

The next week the same thing happened. I showered, went through tests, ate, and rested. If this was an experiment, I was happy to be part of it. Five days later, a German soldier came in and told me I was assigned to work as a tailor for an important officer who would soon return from combat. The nurses gave me proper clothes, unlike the striped prison uniforms, and I was released from the hospital.

The soldier and I got into a waiting car and drove to the outskirts of Dachau, to a small house surrounded by a wall with barbed wire on top of it. We passed through a gate manned by soldiers down a narrow driveway and parked in front of the house. *This must be someplace important*, I thought, seeing a small contingent of soldiers guarding the house and premises. I was taken inside and seated in a small entry hall. I could feel my heartbeat in my wrists and temples. So far, nothing seemed threatening, so I tried to stay calm.

A tall German officer came to the entry hall and told me to follow him. We walked into a study that was furnished with a big desk and many books. He lowered himself into a large leather armchair behind the desk and waved for me to take a seat across from him. Once I was settled, he introduced himself as Colonel Helmut Dietrick.

"Let me get right to the point," he said. "I have been sent here to recuperate from a wound. I am allowed to have my family with me, so they are here as well. I understand you are a tailor."

I nodded as his piercing blue eyes studied me.

"My clothes are in disrepair. You have been assigned to me to put my uniforms into proper military shape. Can you do this?"

The colonel spoke to me in perfect Polish. I was impressed.

"Yes, I can," I answered in the best Polish I could muster.

"Good!" he said with the hint of a smile at the corners of his mouth. "You will be shown to your sleeping quarters, told where you are to eat, and a few other rules of this house. Follow me now, and I will show you what you have to repair and where you will work."

The colonel turned me over to Sigfried, a civilian Pole of German descent who was in charge of the house. He showed me to a small room where I would sleep, then ushered me to a small adjacent room with a sewing machine and everything I would need to do my work. The sight of a workroom with all these materials made my heart race. He nodded for me to follow him, and we went up a flight of stairs to another room with a huge closet filled with the colonel's civilian clothes and uniforms. He told me to look over the uniforms, then select three of them and take them back to the sewing room and do my work. Sigfried explained the procedures and timing for all meals and the other house rules.

I was very happy to be inside, to be warm and clean and fed, yet I felt some guilt about Yankel and the other inmates I had been working with. Who could know I would be in this position because of a *Kapo*'s hat and the audacity of my friend.

Each day I worked on the uniforms, trying not to go too fast. I didn't want this dream to end. Sigfried constantly checked on me, not only to make sure I was doing my job, but to satisfy his growing interest in how I made beauty from rags. I saw the colonel's wife and children at times. She would usually nod at me as she walked past. He had two children, a girl of about 11 years old and a boy of about 9 years old. The two would come to the sewing room sometimes to watch me work. They never spoke, although I think they wanted to.

One day, to my surprise, Colonel Dietrick appeared. He had never paid me a visit in my workplace. He told me to stay seated, then asked how I was doing.

"I am doing well." I smiled. "I hope you are satisfied with my work."

"Yes, I am," he said in an approving tone. Then, he asked me where I was from. I told him. He asked me if I could read, and I nodded.

"Do you like to read?"

"I do. I miss reading very much."

He thought for a minute and replied, "*Ach so,* I will arrange with Sigfried to allow you to read one book at a time from the library here. Some books are in Polish, and some are in German. Can you read German?"

I answered that I could.

His eyes widened in surprise for a moment, and he replied, "That is very good." A full smile—the first I'd ever seen from him—lit up his face. "Yes, that is very good." He nodded and left.

When he was out of sight, I let out a long sigh of relief and continued my work.

Talking with the Colonel

One day, the colonel came into the sewing room, his second visit ever. I hoped nothing was wrong, and wondered why he was there. He asked me how I was doing.

"Very well. I enjoy working, and it pleases me to improve the condition of your uniforms."

The colonel seemed to visibly relax from his usual officer-like posture and leaned forward, closer to me. "Avrum, after this war is over, do you know what you will do?"

I wasn't sure where this conversation was leading and how honest I should be—or could afford to be. I decided to be honest, but careful. "Sir, it's hard for me to imagine the end of this nightmare."

He nodded and waited for a moment, as though he was thinking about my answer. Before I could continue, he said, "Make no mistake. This war will end. German soldiers are becoming younger as well as older. We are running out of well-trained troops. There are subcamps with factories throughout Europe and especially in Germany that are making war products like munitions and weapons. The Americans and British regularly bomb them. The workers are mostly Jews and when one dies, they are replaced by another." The colonel searched my face for a reaction and continued. "The supply of workers seems endless, but the Americans and British, and the Russians too, keep advancing. The workers also somehow know what is happening. The efficiency at the factory gets continually worse, even with the steps taken to make the workers fear for their lives if they don't produce better. Yes, it is only a matter of time." The colonel stopped and sighed. "But you haven't answered my question."

"Colonel," I said, "I am hopeful that my parents will survive, but common sense tells me that I will probably never see them again. My focus in life is to survive and find my sister, Lena. She is a little younger than I am, and I have a strong feeling that I will see her again. I think of her all the time. She motivates me to not give up." I stopped and wondered if I'd gone too far, if I'd trusted the colonel too much with such personal thoughts.

He said, "We will keep any discussions we have to ourselves, only the two of us. Hopefully, we will have a chance to talk again." He rose, showed me rare smile, and left.

I thought about what he had told me. It was a lot to think about. I was shocked that the colonel had spoken to me so honestly about the weaknesses of the German war machine and the impossible idea of their defeat. He was an officer and an aristocrat. I was only a Jewish craftsman whose future looked dim. Yet, here he was, trusting me with his fears and concerns. I supposed he had to purge himself and get unspoken worries off his chest.

It occurred to me that perhaps there were more like him. If so, what did that mean, if anything? He didn't seem to be worried that I would tell anyone, but then, who would I tell? Who could I tell? No one. The colonel and I were bonded in a strange way. I could not grasp the level of his frustration in his situation. What could he do about the feelings he had? It was encouraging to feel his trust in me and I did my best to understand and to appreciate it. I had once been told that war made strange bedfellows. I never understood that idea until this moment.

My thoughts drifted to Lena. I trusted, in my mind, that she was safe. I could only hope that was true. *Please, God, let the war and the suffering end.*

The Colonel

Colonel Helmut Dietrick climbed into bed with his wife, Marta, a striking blue-eyed, blonde woman of slender stature. It had been a long day, and it felt good to relax his body on the clean sheets. His wife looked up from the book she was reading and studied his face for a long time. "Dear, are you all right?"

He sighed. "You know, *Liebchen*, I was thinking. My father fought in World War I at the battle of Verdun. My grandfather was a soldier before him. And here I am, continuing the family tradition, an officer in the German army, yet it makes me unhappy to be doing so. It shouldn't, but it does. What we—and by 'we' I mean Germans—are doing to the Jews is wrong and distasteful. There is no rational reason for our inhumane actions. In my own battalion, I had two Jews serving."

"Jews in the German army?"

"Yes, Jews serving their country because they were being loyal Germans. So, it seems okay to use them however it suits us, while on the other hand we are killing them like flies. I just find that hard to live with."

She neither agreed nor disagreed as she waited for him to finish his thoughts.

"Look at our tailor, young Avrum. I tell you he is a decent fellow who has lost his whole family except for his sister, who he has vowed to find and become reunited with. She is the only remaining member of his family. I would not be disappointed if our son grew up to be like Avrum."

"Yes, I can see that," she said.

"Our son is a hard and skilled worker, dedicated to his family, educated and kind. I hope he does not follow in my military footsteps. I want him, most of all, to be a good person. Much like Avrum."

She nodded, beginning to understand the greater depth of her husband.

"I leave in a couple weeks for a new assignment. I hope I am fortunate enough to return to you and our children. I very much want to teach and guide them in the right direction of life. Yes, I would be happy to have my son be like Avrum, the tailor."

She smiled in assurance. Her love for her husband and his ideals were so much easier to embrace than the inflexible philosophies of the Third Reich.

"You are the only person in the world I can say this to." He smiled.

She looked deep into his eyes, placed her delicate hand into his, and gave it a soft squeeze. No words were needed.

"Now, my love," the colonel said, "let's turn off the light and get our rest."

5

LENA
OCTOBER 1943 TO DECEMBER 1943

Chaya's Story

Every day was filled with activity. I helped with preparing the meals as well as anything else that needed to be done. I made an effort to get to know each of the partisans around me. Our group was an interesting mix of city Jews and village Jews, most of them under 30 years old. We had doctors, lawyers, engineers and other professionals among us, as well as merchants and money handlers. We had craftsmen and artisans. All around me, I heard several languages being spoken, mostly Polish, Russian, Ukrainian, and Yiddish.

One day, Schmuel and two other partisans brought in two boys and a girl. The two boys had been looking for the partisans when they stumbled upon the girl, Chaya Rabinowicz. Schmuel asked me if I would look after her.

I agreed, and I liked Chaya immediately. She was quiet in the beginning and spoke little but worked hard. She was interested in everything we had to say, and when she spoke, her words were wise beyond her years. She fit in with Irena, Anna, and me quite nicely.

One evening, as a small group of us sat together chatting, Irena asked her, "Chaya, how come you are here with us?"

Chaya took a deep breath, looked around at the eager faces

awaiting her answer, and told us her story. "I lived in a small town named Sanok, about 300 kilometers from Warsaw. My father was a merchant with his own store. I had three sisters and a brother. The Nazis started rounding up Jews, and during the chaos I became separated from my family. I had no idea where they went. Since I was the oldest, and looked like I could work, the Nazis took me to a work camp. I spent some time at one camp, then I was transferred to another one for a short period, until finally they sent me to a camp called Sobibor. By the time I got to Sobibor, I had seen the horrible things the Nazis were doing to the Jews and I had no illusions about what would eventually happen to me. Every day was a day of survival.

"I learned quickly that Sobibor was a death camp, an extermination destination for Jews. The inmates of this camp knew exactly what was going on, but we did not have the means to do anything about it. The average population of inmates was around 600 to 650 prisoners, of which a small number were put in positions that kept the camp running: cooking, cleaning, maintenance and so on. The Germans regularly picked out small groups of sick and underachieving workers from the camp and killed them in their gas chambers. They immediately replaced the exterminated group with new workers that came in regularly on trains. Human turnover and harsh discipline kept all the workers off-balance and prevented rebellion."

We were hypnotized by Chaya's story. This wasn't new to us. We each had our own version of the same tale.

Chaya continued. "In the summer of 1943, I heard talk that we were all going to die. The rumors had plenty of facts behind them to make me fear the worst. The trainloads of Jews still arrived like clockwork but brought fewer numbers every week. I also heard that the Russians were coming closer and that their vengeful treatment of Germans was as barbaric as the Germans' treatment of the Jews. Then, the Nazis closed Belzec, another death camp, and sent its population of about 600 Jews to Sobibor for quick extermination in its gas chambers. One day, a small group of inmates successfully escaped from a work detail in the forest. The Germans, in order to teach the inmates an unforgettable lesson, killed ten prisoners for each inmate that had escaped. Each day was terrifying, never knowing who was to die next. We felt desperate and helpless. The Germans put a minefield around the camp to prevent any thoughts of escaping." Chaya stopped for a moment and took a deep breath.

"Chaya," I asked, "are you alright?"

"Yes, I'm okay." She told us that there had been an attempted escape through a tunnel dug out by the prisoners over many months. The Germans discovered the tunnel and killed 100 workers in reprisal. "We were all saddened and terrified, but we knew that to stay was to die, so why not die trying to escape? There was nothing to lose. We needed hope, something to live for."

She said that that hope came in the form of an idea by a respected inmate Leon Feldhendler, who recognized the need for an escape plan and the importance of finding a leader who could put it all together. Leon directed their attention to Alex Pechersky, a recent arrival who had served as a lieutenant in the Russian Army. Feldhendler knew that they needed someone with some military experience and planning ability to pull off an escape plan. Pechersky seemed to be perfect for the job. Pechersky accepted the challenge, and agreed with Feldhendler that time was very short, but that he could make an escape plan work. They decided to share the plan information with only a few inmates to minimize the odds of betrayal. The planners, in order to avoid reprisals and punishment of their fellow prisoners, felt it was best to leave no one behind, and so decided on a mass escape. Everyone would go at once.

The Escape

"The Escape Committee decided that the plan should be put into action in October, when the commander of the camp, Gustav Wagner—called 'The Beast'—and his assistant would leave for their vacations. As soon as the officers left the camp, the plan would immediately be activated.

"Every day, just before the evening roll call, the SS soldiers and Ukrainian guards overseeing the workshops would make their last checks before locking up. The inmates, who usually stood quietly, staring at the ground during the inspection, would assault the inspectors, kill them, and take their weapons. There would still be SS officers and guards stationed around the camp, but now the inmates would have enough weapons to either fight their way out through the gates or cause a big enough distraction to draw attention away from the escapees as they stormed out of the camp.

The mass escape was scheduled to start at the end of evening roll call, when dusk would limit visibility. Roll call was a good reason to gather the prisoners, so they could move as a force. It would be conducted by prisoners dressed in SS uniforms taken from the officers killed in the workshops. Then, the prisoners would be led to the main gate in an orderly fashion by what appeared to be SS officers. At that point, prisoners would be told to run for their lives through the main gate and out of camp. Those prisoners who'd gotten guns from the dead guards would do their best to shoot the remaining guards and draw attention to themselves, so the Germans would concentrate their fire away from those escaping. There were certain to be inmate deaths, but doing nothing would surely mean the annihilation of everyone in the camp. Attempting to escape was the only logical choice."

We murmured approval to one another.

"On the designated day of the escape, the committee did its job. No one at roll call, except the committee, had any idea what was going on. As planned, the SS soldiers and Ukrainian guards were ambushed, killed and stripped of their weapons. Prisoners gathered and took their position for roll call. Our select inmates, dressed as SS soldiers stood before the prisoners, looking and acting quite like the actual German military. Some inmates had bewildered looks on their faces, confused by how familiar some of the SS guards looked.

"Everything was going according to plan when suddenly the alarm went off. One of the dead SS soldiers had been discovered."

Chaya was talking fast now, almost out of breath. She was animated, looking away from us and speaking loudly. We just sat and listened, not daring to interrupt.

"No one, at that moment, understood what was happening. Then, Pechersky jumped on a table and shouted in Russian, 'This is an escape! We cannot turn back or we'll all be killed! Whoever survives, bear witness to the world and let them know what has happened here!' A roar of voices exploded. Those who didn't understand Russian just followed the mob. I didn't know we had enough strength left for such an outburst of sound and action. Suddenly, the guards started firing. About 400 to 500 prisoners ran to the main gate, and flooded through it, leaving a small number of inmates who were too confused or weak to make such a sudden move.

"My ears were filled with pain from the explosions in the minefields and the sound of grenades, rifles, and machine guns being fired. Bodies were falling all around me. I ran straight towards the German quarters, thinking that there would be less mines there. My legs burned from fatigue, but I just kept on running, keeping my eyes on the woods ahead of me. A few of us made it and pressed on through the trees and soft underbrush. I could hear the terrible sounds of guns and death behind me, but I waited for no one. Eventually, under cover of darkness, I reached a farm and hid in the barn. I took refuge in the sweet-smelling straw and fell asleep. In the early morning, I was awakened by the sound of a rattling pail and sat up. The farmer had come out to milk the cows and discovered me. I froze, fearing the worst, but luck and God were on my side. He was a kind man and very anti-Nazi. He gave me food but said I couldn't stay. It was too dangerous for us both. He told me, however, that he had friends who would help me. I didn't know if he could be trusted, but I had no choice. He kept his word and through his friends, I met the two Jewish partisans who brought me here."

Staying Alive

Schmuel became a regular visitor to my area. He always came to see his sister, but also spent some time with me. I liked spending time with him. He was very busy, as were the other leaders, making sure we had food and creating plans to sabotage the Germans in any way our little partisan group could. We tried to interact with other partisan groups, but most of the Polish partisans were not very friendly when they found out that we were Jews. It was hard to understand their attitude since we were all on the same side, fighting the same enemy. We Jews had done nothing to deserve the Poles' hatred. Weren't we supposed to be fighting the German invaders and destroyers of our Polish homeland together?

According to Schmuel it was because of antisemitism. He said that it had to do with jealousy. The Jews seemed to be better educated and the Polish peasants resented that. He also told me that the Polish Catholic Church held the Jews accountable for the death of Christ. How was that possible?

I asked Schmuel, but he said, "Lena, it isn't worth our time to discuss the ignorance of these people. We have other things to do, like staying alive, staying healthy, and fighting the Germans. There are many Polish people—gentiles and Jews alike—who help us and understand that we all need to fight the Germans. In fact, tomorrow, we're going to get some food from some Polish supporters, or at least I hope so. If you want, I'll take you with us."

I was so excited. I was the first one there when the group gathered in the morning.

Sol was in charge. He told us that we were going to meet with a friendly farmer who had collected food for us. He stressed that we must always be alert, since the Germans dressed some of their soldiers as peasants to act as spies. So we needed to avoid any contact with people outside our group. Sol personally knew this farmer, and he wanted to do his best to not get him in any trouble for helping us.

The plan was to get to the farm and borrow a cart to transport the food back to our camp. Afterwards, we would return the cart. The idea seemed simple enough, as long as we didn't run into any Germans or Nazi sympathizers. It would take all eight of us—including Irena, Chaya, and me—the better part of the day to tramp to the farm and pick up the much-needed food.

Farmer Janusz

It was a long walk to the farm. When we got there, the farmer greeted us warmly. He introduced himself as Janusz, and said he had been expecting us. Sol referred to him as "Jan" when they spoke. We also met his wife, Zofia, who brought us much-welcomed sausage, bread, jam, and two pitchers of milk and water. Farmer Jan introduced us to an older man working on the farm, who he said was a cousin, and two young girls: Catherine and Mollie. He said that his children had gone away, one to Warsaw, the other to serve in the Polish army and had not heard from them in a while. He told us that the cart would be ready to go as soon as we loaded all the food he had gathered for us. Most of the food was stored in the barn, waiting to be transferred. Sol divided us into teams to collect everything and load the cart.

I was partnered with Mollie. She was my age and spoke only a little. It's hard to explain, but I had a strange feeling that I knew her, even though I was sure we had never met before. She was very nice, and I liked her. The more I worked with her, the more I became convinced that she was Jewish. I thought that she certainly must know that she was helping Jewish partisans, so I decided to take a chance and abruptly asked, "Mollie, are you Jewish?"

She stopped and looked at me as if I were pointing a bright light at her, not sure what she could, or would, say. Finally, she said, "Yes, I am Jewish."

"I knew it! I felt something special between us."

Her smile told me she felt the same. She suddenly became vocal. She told me that she and a brother and sister who had escaped from the Germans by jumping from a train carrying Jews to a work camp. She and her family were among them. Her brother and sister had been killed in the escape. She went on about being found by Farmer Jan and praised the kindness of him and his wife. She said that no one else on the farm, except for them, knew that she was Jewish. All the neighbors had been told that she was a distant cousin who came to help them since all their children were away. Occasionally, Germans came, looking for food. Sometimes they paid for it, other times they just took what they wanted.

"Yes, they do that," I said.

I told her how much I liked being with the partisans and told me what little she knew about the German occupation. She told me what she had heard about death camps and how the Germans were always looking Jews. It was frightening to hear, but we went on like two chattering magpies, sharing our stories and information freely as we loaded the food. We, two young Jewish girls, had become old beyond our years. With the cart finally loaded, we all thanked Farmer Jan and his wife and helpers. I gave Mollie a big hug and we parted with tears in our eyes. We were both happy to have had a private moment together, to share our experiences, feelings, and information. I hoped I would get a chance to see her again.

The Jewish Partisans

I was flattered by how often Schmuel visited and the amount of time he spent with me. I'm sure he enjoyed our little group of girls and, especially, his sister. I was also aware that the time he spent with me had been steadily increasing. I felt good about that. Though I was nearly 17 years old, I was really a mature woman. The pressure of the war made everyone grown up faster. It never occurred to me that I missed out on being a typical giggly teenager, a situation shared by most of us who were hiding and surviving in the forest.

Schmuel and I had long talks about all kinds of subjects. There was so much I was curious about. I increasingly bombarded him with questions on all sorts of things. I already knew the answer to some of them, but Schmuel always knew more than I did, and I loved the way he explained things, as well as the sound of his voice.

One evening, I asked him about the other partisan groups in the forest. Were they like ours?

"Some yes, some no," he replied. "Most of them are bigger than our group, and each one has its own goals and style of resistance. Like the group headed by a fellow named Yechiel Grynszpan. His group is very good at saving Jewish lives. He concentrates on those who are stuck in the ghettos. He gets out as many as he can before the Germans come to round them up and take them to a death camp. They feel it's better to avoid a lot of shooting and live another day to save more Jews."

"How do they avoid the shooting?" I asked.

"They do as we do and hide in the forest, only fighting when they must or when they can. You know, there are many Poles who hate

Jews and turn us in when they can, or even try to kill us themselves. It is incomprehensible to be treated that way when it's the Germans who are the enemy, not the Jews. We're lucky that there are Poles who help us get food, clothing, and weapons when they can. I am sure God will reward them. There are also Polish and Russian partisans that I've heard about. Can you believe that some of those groups will not let Jews fight with them?"

"Why not? We're on the same side. It makes no sense."

"I agree, it's absolutely insane. Those units are way better equipped than we are because they get some supplies from the Russians. They have more of everything except, of course, lice and scabs."

I giggled and nodded.

"However, in the end, we are all doing what we can to disrupt the Germans," Schmuel added. "Blowing up trains, telephone poles, and bridges should be the goal of all partisan groups."

"I like that," I said.

"I heard from a Russian partisan that there is a Marshall Tito in the Yugoslav area who fights the Germans man-to-man and has actually won some battles. He also told me stories about the Russians advancing and actually defeating the Germans, making them run in retreat. God help us, I pray this disaster is over soon and we can search for our families."

"We all pray for that," I said.

He yawned and stretched out his arms. "It's time to go to sleep and prepare ourselves for another day."

Schmuel's advice to get sleep and prepare for the next day always meant that the conversation was over. I found those words to be a special, intimate end to my day.

Back in Camp

The trip to the farm was really good for me. Camp life had become dull and monotonous. It was also literally crawling with difficulty. The lice were horrible. No matter where we moved, from one campground to another, there they were. They either greeted us there or followed us on the journey. They carried filth and disease, especially typhoid, which were major problems in some of the partisan camps.

We had to keep moving, as the Germans searched for us, day and night, always on our heels. In the winter, we made shelters, using whatever was available in the forest, or any materials we could find around farms and the outskirts of villages, towns, and cities. The Russians called these makeshift shelters *zemlyankas*, which means "dugout" in Russian. We hunkered down in these dugouts to stay warm. Though they each held a good number of people, some partisans couldn't stand the crush of so many people and chose to stay out in the winter weather, even though they were poorly clothed and miserable from the cold. Then, when we were finally settled and comfortable, the leaders would announce that we had to move to stay ahead of the Germans. It was a never-ending cycle.

One evening, Schmuel came to visit with me. We spent a pleasant time together talking about frivolous things. Though we joked and laughed, I was bothered by an idea that nibbled away at me. Finally, I told him that I needed to talk to him before he left. He asked what was on my mind.

"I know you are planning some sabotage and I want to go with you. I can help."

"Lena," he said, "yes, we are planning something, but this will be very dangerous."

"I can do my part, Schmuel. I am healthy and strong, and I want to fight the Germans. Please give me a chance."

He told me he would speak to the leader of the Sabotage Committee, Abe Zorin, about my request and that he would get back to me the following day. I didn't know much about the mission, but I wanted to be a part of it. Our group, like other partisan groups, had destroyed bridges and power plants, as well as power lines. We had stolen food and medical supplies headed to the Germans and blown up trains loaded with troops and armaments. I wanted to be part of that.

The next day I received my answer. Schmuel told me that he had three pieces of good news for me.

"Yes?" I said, thrilled to hear any good news. "Tell me."

He smiled and said that I was approved to go on the mission.

"Wonderful!" *That's one piece of news*, I thought. *But he said there were three.* "And what are the other two pieces of news?"

"You'll have the company of Irena. And Anna. You're all to be ready right after dinner."

I couldn't have been more delighted... and nervous.

The Train

After dinner, 12 of us—nine men and three women—met at a separate location, away from the others. The men had been on missions before, but Irena, Anna, and I had not. Schmuel introduced us to Abe Zorin, who was in charge of the operation. Abe looked more like a math professor than a partisan. He was thin but wiry and wore thick glasses. He greeted the group, and then gave us a general rundown on the plan. The men nodded their heads as Abe spoke. The ladies just listened, trying to absorb every detail. Abe emphasized that we were about to go on a risky, but enormously important mission. He said that the darkness of evening would help to hide our activities. We were going to blow up a German train carrying supplies, as well as German soldiers. We glanced around at one another in wide-eyed excitement.

Abe told us the train's schedule and said that there would be German soldiers walking the tracks as protection against sabotage. Our plan was to sneak up close to the train tracks and quietly plant the explosives under them. After the men placed the explosives and set the fuses, they'd sneak back through the tall grass and run away. The rest of us would be waiting in the grass and leave with them before a German patrol could see us. They told us girls to keep on the lookout for German soldiers and warn the men placing the explosives if the guards got too close. We were each given a weapon. The men, additionally, were given explosives. It was time to act.

It seemed like a long walk to the tracks, which ran along the edge of the forest. My heart throbbed in my mouth. I was very alert, aware of every little sound. We finally reached our destination, a raised trestle with easy access to the tracks. We were relieved to see a clear landscape before us, with no guards in sight. Now the plan began to pick up momentum.

The girls and I spread out evenly, each about 50 meters apart, watching out for German guards, to make sure they didn't surprise any of us. The men hurried to the trestle, placed the explosives, and retreated to safer ground. As we all moved away in the tall grass, we could hear the train coming. We stopped and lay down at a distance of almost 150 meters from the tracks. Two German soldiers appeared and stood at the edge of the trestle. My body tensed up as a smoking locomotive pulling a long train of cars approached, the clacking sound of the wheels getting louder and louder. The German soldiers stepped back from the trestle to a safer distance from the oncoming train. I lay in the grass, holding my breath, praying everything would work out as planned, worried that some little thing would go wrong.

Then, suddenly, as the engine passed the soldiers, the explosives blew up with a huge and deafening roar. The explosion filled the night with an intense blinding light. I heard the loud screeching of steel wheels on steel tracks. Then, with delight, I watched the engine slide off the tracks, taking the rest of the train with it, car after car twisting and breaking apart. I stared, fascinated. Schmuel's barking voice broke the trance, telling us to run like hell back into the forest. We needed no further persuasion and took off.

We ran and ran until we were finally out of breath. Then we slowed down and made our way back to camp, feeling protected by the darkness of the night. The girls and I went to our beds, but it took a long time for us to fall asleep. The excitement and drama of the night played in my mind over and over. I was thrilled to have done my part against the Germans and ached to have another opportunity to fight them again.

After the Sabotage

We were all ecstatic after we blew up the German train. We were fighting back as Jews. Our Partisan group had a lot in common with other similar groups. We were not trained to be rebels, but here we were. Using what little resources we had, we showed the Germans that we could contribute in the fight against them. Schmuel and the other leaders were concerned about what the Germans would do after such a heavy blow: the loss of a train, soldiers, and supplies. They also had to rebuild the trestle and the tracks.

We were told to pack up and prepare to move deeper into the forest, where we would be harder to find. We knew that the Germans hated coming into the forest because it was the domain of the partisans, and they couldn't use army vehicles. Tanks and personnel trucks were too large to negotiate through and around the trees. Smaller vehicles were easier targets for guerilla warfare. Still, we picked up as we were told and made our way through the trees and thick forest growth to another temporary place.

We always deployed guards around our perimeter to protect the camp from a surprise attack. Early one morning, we heard airplanes overhead, more than usual. It made us all quite nervous. We only had a meager supply of guns and ammunition, which limited how well we could respond and how long we could hold out in a fire fight. Suddenly, one of our lookouts came running into camp, frantically. "Germans in the forest!" he shouted.

The entire camp sprang into frenzied action. We quickly packed whatever we could and started to move the camp when the first mortar shells rained down on us. We heard the Germans firing on our lookouts, who were firing back. Above us, German Stuka dive bombers appeared and started dropping bombs around us. The dive bombers made a hideous screaming sound as they released their vessels of death, killing some of our fellow partisans and destroying the forest that had been our home. Pieces of trees flew through the air, along with huge clumps of earth. Totally disorganized, we ran for cover, for our lives. Irena and Chaya ran with me. I had no idea where everyone else had gone. Some of our group hunkered down behind tree stumps and fallen logs, shooting at the Germans as they advanced closer. The gun and cannon fire were deafening, and gun smoke was everywhere, filling our lungs and burning our eyes. The mortars continually exploded all around us, throwing up large showers of dirt. The German advance slowed up and then seemed to stop, but the mortars continued. One that landed almost on top of our position, exploded, and splattered us with dirt.

"Chaya! Irena! Are you alright?" I shouted.

Chaya shouted back, "Yes, I'm okay, but Irena has been hit!"

I scrambled over to where Irena lay against a log, shouting as I ran, "Irena, Irena, are you all right?"

She didn't move or respond. She just lay there motionless, her head bleeding profusely.

Chaya grabbed my arm and in a choked voice said, "Lena, Irena cannot answer. She's dead."

"No!" I cried. "That can't be."

When I looked at Irena again, I saw that Chaya was right. A piece of shrapnel from a mortar had struck her in the temple and killed her. My wonderful friend was no more. I was devastated. How would Schmuel take this? I became suddenly aware that even the mortar fire had stopped, which meant the Germans were withdrawing. The small arms fire continued, sporadic at first, then fading away. While teams of partisans fired from hidden positions, driving the Germans back, our leaders checked everywhere, taking a count of the fallen. Six of our group, including Irena, had died. Though we suffered a small number of casualties considering the scale of the battle and size of the German force, we found no comfort in our meager loss. To us, every life was precious. Schmuel was thoroughly devastated upon hearing of Irena's death. He found us and knelt next to his precious sister for a long time, quietly weeping.

Meir showed up quite suddenly, having heard of the situation, and dropped to his knees at his brother's side, weeping with Schmuel at the loss of their sister.

Then Schmuel stood up, looked at us with firm resolution and said, "We shall take the bodies of our friends into the forest, bury them, and say Kaddish."

"Amen," Meir whispered.

We picked up the weapons of the fallen, gathered whatever was still useful, and made our way deeper into the forest, each of us silently mourning for those who died.

6

AVRUM
NOVEMBER 1943 TO MARCH 1944

To Camp

Spending my days sewing repairs on uniforms in the home of the colonel felt almost like a normal life. The family treated me with an unexpected amount of respect and decency, which went a long way to heal my injured mind. The work made me feel productive and they fed me quite well, which put some weight on me. I no longer looked like a death camp prisoner. I worked just fast enough to appear skilled as a tailor and just slow enough to lengthen my stay in the home, all the time hoping against hope that this situation would allow me to continue to survive.

One day, I noticed a lot of activity taking place in the house. A chill ran through me when I saw the family making preparations to move out. I wasn't surprised when Sigfried came to my room and told me to follow him. He took me to the study, where the colonel was stuffing a leather traveling bag with some of the uniforms I had repaired.

As I entered the room, the colonel straightened up and smiled warmly at me. He dismissed Sigfried, instructing him to close the door after himself. Now, with the two of us alone, he turned to me. "Avrum," he addressed me by my given name as I stared down at my tattoo, "my family and I will be leaving soon. I have been reassigned. You have done a splendid job with my uniforms and I am quite pleased." His smile faded into a painful expression. "I have no choice but to return you to your previous situation. The decision is not mine. However, I want to tell you in this study, between you and me, that you must be brave, and outlive the war. Germany is losing. This is an unnecessary war and an embarrassment to the German people. I am sickened by the display of cruelty our country's leaders have shown the whole world." He stood erect, reached out, and shook my hand.

I was choked up with emotion and could only say, "Thank you for your fairness and kindness. I wish you and your family the best."

He nodded and motioned to the door. I turned and went back to my room. I sat down and fell into deep thought. Before I came here, I hated every German. But there was nothing to hate about the colonel and his family. It's the Nazis that hate. The sickness of "hate" belongs to them. This was a valuable lesson: to judge each person on their own merit. I thought to myself, *Avrum, at least you are healthier than you have been in some time. Keep your head up and focus on surviving and finding Lena.* Finally, my thoughts drifted off to a peaceful place. I was humming my mother's song, when a knock on the door interrupted me. My ride back to camp had come to pick me up.

Returning to Camp

As I got into the car that would return me to the work camp, I considered my situation. When I had left my work detail to go to the colonel's home, I was weak and getting sicker every day. After being in the hospital and then spending time at the house repairing the colonel's uniforms, I had regained my strength and my mind was refreshed. I thought about my parents and little Lena. It was dismal to think of Momma and Poppa, knowing what went on in the camps. I never gave up hope that they were alive, but was constantly nagged by what I felt could be the horrible truth. I thought about Lena and my responsibility to find her. I felt that she needed me, and I definitely needed to know she was safe, wherever she might be.

I felt a jerking halt as the car stopped at the main gate. I was turned over to a soldier who took me to a different barrack than the one I had left. I looked around me, searching for Yankel or someone I might know, but saw no one familiar.

The new barrack was filled with gaunt, starving people, and I felt oddly out of place. The *Kapo* looked me up and down with his usual bullying glare and I immediately reverted to familiar camp behavior, making sure to avoid any eye contact. I was shown to my bed and ordered to climb in and go to sleep. I did as I was told and lay there, awake, for a few hours, waiting for the morning.

I fell right back into the old routine the next morning, which started with roll call, of course. I was put on a work detail in the position of a *Sonderkommando*, a prisoner whose job it was to remove bodies of murdered Jews from the gas chambers and bury them in a big pit. I had never done that before. With so much suffering and death in the camp, most of us suppressed our emotions—a necessity if we were to live through this ordeal. Now, however, I felt a new tightness in my mind and body. I, along with other *Sonderkommandos*, had to untangle stiff, naked corpses that were interlocked with one another, gripping anything around them in their last moments of life, clinging to each other desperately. The looks frozen on their faces told terrible stories.

We loaded the bodies onto carts and hauled them to a mass grave dug out by a bulldozer. There, we threw the bodies into the pit, one by one, and covered them with lye, ashes, and sand. Men, women, and children became a pile of human refuse, dusted with chemicals to make them dissolve without too much foul odor. I was finally able to shut my mind down when I thought about what the colonel had told me. "The Germans were losing the war," he had said. I let that thought comfort me as I did my job.

Every day was surreal. Not only were we burying corpses, but we could see the smoke from the crematoriums. The Germans were doing their best to destroy the evidence of their bestiality as quickly as they could. Having returned to long hours and little food, I was getting weaker daily, and it worried me. I didn't know how long I could survive, if at all. If a miracle didn't happen soon, I would be one of those bodies.

Then, once again,, opportunity came at the most unexpected time. One morning, at the end of roll call, a German soldier appeared and loudly addressed the prisoners.

"Who is a carpenter?" he shouted.

I quickly raised my hand.

"I need six carpenters!" he went on, as he scanned the prisoners.

I looked around and saw that many had their hands raised.

He pointed from one raised hand to another and another, saying, "You and you and you and..."

My spirits sank as he picked one prisoner after another. I stood, my hand still raised high, at the far end of the group of prisoners. Then he wheeled about, looked in my direction and, surprisingly, pointed his finger at me. "And you."

A wave of relief washed over me. He continued until he had his six carpenters. Then he motioned with a wave of his arm, turned away from us, and commanded "Follow me!"

The chosen men immediately stepped out of the roll call group and followed him. The man walking beside me leaned toward me and asked in a hushed tone, "Are you really a carpenter?"

I responded, "Are you?"

He smiled and we walked on.

Some of the barracks were terribly run down and needed a variety of repairs. We were given tools and told what needed to be done. Then we got to work. I had hoped that we'd have real carpenters in the group who we could either follow by example, or who were okay with telling us what to do and how to do it.

When we arrived at the barracks, those who knew little of carpentry made sure to work next to someone who knew something. Through watching and occasional whispers back and forth, the amateurs among our group learned quickly and looked like they knew what they were doing. I got through my first day doing a pretty good imitation of a carpenter, without losing any fingers. That night, I was put in a different barrack, along with the other carpenters and some craftsmen who did jobs around the camp. I immediately noticed the improvement of the food. Actually, it wasn't much better, but we got a little more than other prisoners. I was also happy to get away from handling dead people and worked hard to detach myself from that horrific duty. I felt an invigorating surge of energy to survive.

Itzhak

The attrition of the workers was dramatic. The malnutrition and deterioration of the men—results of the long hours, heavy workload, and the abuse of the *Kapos*—combined to destroy the spirit and, eventually, the person. As the prisoner ranks shrunk, new workers arrived by train or truck. One day, we received some new replacements from the Lvov Ghetto in Poland. Among them I met Itzhak Berman, a rabbi who had a business that sold religious items such as tallises, tefellins, and menorahs. The closure of the synagogues and the penalty of death imposed on all Jewish practices had put him out of business. He lived in hiding with a family for a while until he was seized in a Nazi roundup. Now he found himself in our camp and in my barrack. I liked him immediately and we quickly became friends.

Kapos were brutes, and ours was no different. A mean and sadistic bully, he immediately picked out Itzhak to punish and abuse when the opportunity presented itself. The cruel treatment slowly wore Itzhak out, but he somehow found the resources to keep on going. We often talked.

One evening, he asked me why the Germans were doing such inhumane things to the Jews, as well as the Gypsies, and some of the Poles.

I told him I didn't know. Then I asked him, "Do you still believe in God?"

"Oh yes, of course."

"Then, why does God allow such horrible things to happen to his chosen people?"

He didn't hesitate to answer. "It's not God doing these things. It's the Germans."

"Yes, but can't He stop them?"

"I don't know," Itzhack sighed. "He puts people on earth, and I think He expects them to manage themselves in an appropriate way. Their reward is His blessing and the peace and happiness they find within themselves for doing the right thing. The Nazis are an unhappy group, in my opinion, who are trying to find acceptance. I believe that one day, God, in His wisdom, will have His reckoning with them."

"I hope so," I said. "And I hope it's sooner than later."

"From your mouth to God's ear," he answered.

We then sat in silence, enjoying the refreshment of our conversation.

The days passed with a monotonous rhythm, one day after another. The weather had turned colder and our skimpy uniforms provided little or no protection from the elements. Complaining used to keep us warm, but we no longer did that. As we marched to work, I noticed that there were other people besides Jews in our camp, but they were kept in a different location, away from us. As we passed by the women's section, we felt anxious, because upon arrival at the camp, our *Kapo* had forbidden us to look at women at any time. So we kept our eyes on the ground as we marched along, never looking directly at them, but still aware of the women.

One typically cold morning our *Kapo* woke us up early with his usual annoying shout. "Get ready! Get ready now!"

We awoke and prepared ourselves for another day. After a long roll call, we were given a piece of bread and a liquid they called coffee. It tasted disgusting, but at least it was hot. Then we marched to work. I noticed that Itzhak was having a hard time keeping up. I hoped he was all right but feared the worst.

Discussion with Itzhak

One day, Itzhak asked me what the difference was between a German and a Nazi. "Well," I said, "I don't think every German is a Nazi, but all Nazis are German. In Italy, I think they call Nazis 'Fascists', but many Italians do not believe in that doctrine."

"Why are the Nazis so cruel?" he asked.

"I think it's partly because they can be. They're bullies, and bullies almost always get their way. They've lost all concept of human respect and have become blind to everything except their own selfish, warped views. Their judgment day will come."

Itzhak nodded. He was a gentle and kind person who believed in the goodness of his fellow man. It was hard for him to grasp the violence and evil that surrounded us. "Avrum," he asked, "why does Hitler hate us?"

"He hates everyone and everything that isn't German and isn't the way he thinks things should be," I replied. "He even hates some of his own German people, especially those who disagree with him."

"Does he really think he can kill all the Jewish people in the entire world? I mean, there are Jews in so many different countries around the world. Jews are everywhere and they're good citizens wherever they are. Even though they're scattered around the world, don't you think they can help us and maybe rescue us?"

"I think they are trying, but..."

"Do you think they know what is going on here?"

"That's a good question." I looked at his worn, thin face, his hollow, sunken eyes, and worried. "Now lie down, my friend. You need to rest."

"Thank you, Avrum," he whispered. He lowered his head, heaved a weary sigh, and closed his eyes. He never awoke.

Mendel

There was always movement in the camp, as inmates died and were replaced. This was part of our cycle of life, which should really be called "cycle of death."

One dreary day in fall, a new transport arrived, delivering workers from another camp. A few months earlier, Itzhak had died, only to be replaced by a deaf Ukrainian who died a few days later. A fellow named Mendel took the place of the Ukrainian and was assigned the sleeping rack where Itzhak used to lie. I immediately liked him. He had grown up in the small village of Rudki in eastern Poland. He was slightly older than me and had a certain energy about him that separated him from the other workers.

He told me that he was doing better than a lot of workers, because the village he came from was so poor that he often suffered from hunger. Living conditions in his village were difficult and not up to the same standards as cities. The workers who came from the cities were not used to anything close to the substandard conditions under which we labored. Mendel felt that they were not as mentally and physically prepared as he was for what they had to go through.

I told him that it was very frustrating being closely guarded in camp. "We're powerless, unable to do anything to slow Germany down from conquering the world and killing every Jew they can find."

"You and I are doing our part, Avrum," he replied. "Because we're in this camp, these bastards have to have soldiers here to guard us to make sure we don't cause trouble. Every guard watching us is one less soldier on the front line, one less gun to kill the allies and murder Jews. And remember, we are growing more lice than the Germans can deal with!"

We both laughed. It felt good.

He asked me about my family. It was hard to talk about them, because I had no way of knowing what had happened to my mother and father or the rest of my family. My parents were from an older generation, so they were separated from those who were younger. At first I had hope for them, but after I had seen how the Germans divided the men from the women in camps, I couldn't imagine them surviving. Not without each other. Not at their age.

I told Mendel that my big hope was for this war to end so I could find my sister. "My father had left her with a Polish family he trusted, and I can only hope she is safe."

I told Mendel about the song our mother used to sing to us. I sang it softly to him, even though it was hard to do, because I was choked up by the memories and emotions the song stirred up. He thanked me, and then, exhausted, I fell into a deep sleep.

Before I knew it, it was the next morning. After roll call, we had breakfast: the usual piece of bread, and this time a different version of coffee, which tasted like roasted acorns. It was a different kind of awful.

Today, a trainload of Jews arrived at the camp. I hated this regular event because it was the beginning of a process that led to the death of so many of the new arrivals. Though the Germans oversaw the handling of the new workers, veteran inmates were required to help with the actual processing. The German officer in charge had the new workers separated into groups of men, women, children, young, old, potentially good workers, and those who had no value. Then he ordered the veteran inmates to take all valuables from the arrivals. Later, all new prisoners were stripped of their clothes, were issued prison uniforms, and got shaved. Finally, a few specialists tattooed a number on the forearm of each person. At that moment, the new arrival went from being a human to just a number.

That night, Mendel told me that the camps were supposed to show a profit, like a regular business.

"Are you kidding me?" I said. "You mean, you really believe this camp, with all its cruelty and suffering, is a business? You say they want to show a profit while they shower us with grief and exterminate Jews and anyone else they don't like?"

He stepped back, as if accused of lying. "Well, that's what I heard."

It had been a long and hard day and we needed to give our minds a rest. Tomorrow would come all too soon.

The War Wears On

The routine never seemed to change. It was get up early, stand at attention for hours at roll call, eat whatever they gave us, and then trudge off to work. The work hours seemed endless. Then, back to camp, another roll call, eat, and off to our barracks. Prisoners died working on the job. They died going to and coming from work, mostly from health problems, starvation, and abuse.

There were always new workers coming in from many different places. This last week, we got a load of Jews from Germany and a few Italians. They came in trucks instead of cattle cars, which was a little unusual. Some of the new arrivals were assigned to our barrack.

I quickly became friends with a German fellow named Ezra. He had been to other camps, which was fascinating to discuss. We spoke to each other in Yiddish. Ezra brought us news of fighting going on between the Americans and British allies against the Germans. He told us the Germans were getting pushed back and that the Italians were quitting. He had escaped from his previous work camp but had the bad luck to get caught a week later. He told us that while he was outside the work camp, before he was recaptured, he had seen some trucks from the Jewish Brigade Group.

"Jewish Brigade Group?" I asked, astonished at those words appearing in one sentence. It sounded so foreign. All of us gathered around him and said we did not know what that was. Ezra explained that they were soldiers from Palestine, trained by the British, who fought against the Germans. "The soldiers were all Jewish, and every one of them wore an arm patch that said 'Jewish Brigade Group' with a yellow Star of David. Not only that, these Palestinians were trying to help whatever Jews they ran into, whenever it was possible."

We were all thrilled to hear this news. In our dark world of impossibilities, it felt like God had awakened and decided to do something about our situation. It lifted our spirits dramatically.

Two nights later, Ezra and I were talking. I told him that it occurred to me that before the Germans came with their sick plan to kill all the Jews in the world, we were flourishing. "I mean, I know that in many of the Polish cities Jews made up as much as 40 percent of the population. Even though many of the Poles were prejudiced against us, the Jewish communities grew and had become an important part of the economy. Jews also served in the army, and some held public office. We bothered no one and went about our business. I know the Jews also prospered in many other European countries, as well as Russia, Latvia, Lithuania, Romania, Hungary, and so on. There must be something special about us that enables us to prosper despite being disliked by so many."

Ezra thought about that for a minute and said, "I need to think about that. You know, when a Jew meets another Jew, no matter what country they are from, they are instantly family. They were all raised pretty much the same way, with the same thoughtful values, and they understand each other. They are educated in Torah. They all honor Shabbos and the family dinner held on that night and break a piece of matzoh on Passover. We honor and respect each other as Jews and human beings. I think many gentiles live similarly to the way we do, but the Germans, more specifically, the Nazis, live on hate and cannot function in this world as honorable people. We are honorable people and they are not. Look where that got us." Ezra could only shake his head and stare at the ground.

7

LENA
APRIL 1944 TO MAY 1945

The Twerskis

After the German attack, the atmosphere in our group was gloomy. We all deeply felt the loss of our fellow partisans. We were one family and to us, every life, every individual, was precious. It hurt, but there was no time to mourn. We had to pick up the pieces and move on.

Two days later, I heard a commotion on the outskirts of our camp and ran toward the sound, weapon at the ready. It was only our guards bringing in three young men. We all gathered around as Schmuel, Sol, and Meir came forward and took charge. The young men were all about six feet tall and resembled one another. They had weapons and were wearing shabby coats, shirts, and pants, just like us. So they sort of resembled us, as well. Schmuel addressed the three of them. "Who are you?"

The tallest stepped forward. "We are the Twerskis. My name is Yudel. This is my brother, Samuel, and that is our cousin, Mordechai."

A low murmur ran through our group. I could hear some of them muttering 'Twerski' to one another with some sort of surprise or reverence.

Yudel continued. "We came from the east. Our families are mostly Hasidic rabbis, ultra-Orthodox, as you may know."

"What brings you here?" Schmuel asked.

"My brother, cousin, and I decided that we cannot follow the pacifistic philosophy of our forefathers at this time. We feel that it is our duty to save as many Jews as possible, even if it means killing to do so. There are many like us, all dedicated to saving our brethren."

"What news can you give us?"

"Well," Yudel answered, "we have come a long way. On our journey we've learned that there are Jews from many different places who fight wherever they can and with whatever they have available. They can be very different, and yet all have a common purpose. Some are healthy, some are sick, some are hopeful, some are hopeless. What they have in common is poor food, ragtag clothes, and a lack of quality weapons and munitions. They especially have the desire to fight back and survive."

We all nodded in agreement.

"You may have heard of Tuvia Bielski and his brothers."

Most of us had heard of these brothers and considered them examples of how we should think and act.

"They save Jews," Yudel went on. "They even go into the ghettos and sneak out out the Jews who are willing to join our Partisan family and bring them safely back to the forest. Tuvia says that it is more important to save a Jew than to kill a German."

I could feel the heat of emotion rise in our group. Many of us agreed.

"Coming west, Sam, Mordechai, and I tried to join different partisan groups, but most of them won't tale in Jews. Can you believe that?"

"Oh my God," I said to the partisan next to me. "It's unbelievable. What's wrong with them? Can't they see we're all fighting for the same cause?"

"Apparently not. Some can't figure out who is the bigger enemy: the Jews or the Germans. That's called irony." Yudel's voice raised in anger. "But that's not the only problem facing Jews who want to join the fight. Some partisan groups with Jews are communist, in which we have no interest. However, the Germans are losing now. The Russians, with aid from the West, are advancing. There are Zionists recruiting Jews for Palestine. How they will get there I do not know."

Sol stepped forward and asked, "How did you find us? What do you expect from us?"

Yudel spoke in a calm, but firm voice. "Partisans from different groups know enough about other Jewish groups for us to be able to find the general area where they hide and live. We put all the pieces of information and rumors together and got lucky in finding your group."

Sol's face looked pleased but also worried; if these three found us, why couldn't the Germans find us, as well. He whispered something to Schmuel, who answered him softly, but loud enough for some of us to hear.

"They're Twerskis. Very smart. I'm not surprised that they figured it out."

Yudel went on. "Samuel, Mordechai, and I are part of with a small partisan brigade that needs help. We know the location of a German base that's loaded with things we need and things we need to blow up. There are a lot of weapons, munitions, food, and clothing, plus invaluable medical supplies. We need help to take care of that business. That's where you come in. We will share whatever we can get away with after we destroy the base. However, we must do it before they move to another location or shut down."

Schmuel looked at Sol and Meir, who both nodded. Then he said, "Get some rest and we will share whatever food we have. Tomorrow, we will make a plan."

The Other Partisans

Many in our camp knew a great deal about the Twerski family history and shared that knowledge with the rest of us. The Twerskis were a highly respected ultra-Orthodox family from Chernoble. I learned that in the middle of the 18th century, Czar Nicholas of Russia decreed that all Jews had to have last names. At that time, every Jew in Chernobyl did not have a last name. Instead, a Jew established his or her identity by saying the word 'ben' in between his first name, then his father's name and, finally, his grandfather's name. 'Ben' means 'the son of'. So a man's name could be Aaron ben Moisha ben Avrum, which meant 'Aaron, son of Moisha, son of Avrum.' To honor the decree of the Czar and create a last name, a famous rabbi in Chernobyl, Rabbi Menachem Nochum, known as 'the Rabbi of Chernobyl,' named himself after the nearby town of Tweria. He added 'sky' to the end of his name, which means 'a resident of.' The result was the last name of Twersky: a resident of Tweria. That rabbi had eight sons, all of whom became rabbis as well, each establishing his own rabbinical dynasty. Twerskys spread out well beyond Chernobyl to other cities and countries. The ones who came to Poland changed the "y" to an "i", which is very Polish. It seemed like nearly every Twersky or Twerski was a rabbi.

We were uplifted by these Twerskis. They were positive and enthusiastic, which gave us hope. Their visit took us out of the funk we were in from the horrible German attack on us. The news that the Germans were losing the war and the Russians were advancing towards us gave us new energy. Schmuel announced to the rest of the camp that our leaders planned to coordinate with the Twerskis' partisan group. This brought about a feeling of purpose in each and every one of us. Even though our supplies were severely limited and food and clothing sparse, we felt a rush of excitement from the announcement. Our leaders chose a committee to meet with the Twerskis' partisans. The committee and our leaders left with the Twerskis to make plans with their group.

A week later, our committee returned. We were anxious to hear about the meeting and if we were really going to attack the German base together. We never had a cooperative venture with another group of partisans before. All of us gathered at a big fire and Schmuel rose to tell us what was going on. "Fellow partisans, I have exciting news to tell you. As you know, the Twerskis took us to their group, and we met with their leaders. Their group is twice or three times our size."

Eyes widened as we looked excitedly at one another, making enthusiastic facial gestures and whispers of approval and delight.

"They are all Jewish, but a very diversified mix. Some come from the ghetto, some have escaped from work or death camps. There are several communists among them. There are also Zionists who want to go to Palestine. They are mostly Polish, but there are also a few Ukrainians and Latvians, as well as a couple of Russians. However, I remind you, they are all Jews and have committed to fight with a cooperative, single-minded purpose against the Germans. We made plans with them to attack a German supply depot that has things we desperately need for our own survival, but it will take both of our groups working together to accomplish our mission. This German depot has plenty of guns, ammunition, health supplies, food and clothing."

Every face in the group brightened up.

"We have agreed on a meeting place. Tomorrow, we will pack up and join forces with them. Save your questions for tomorrow. You have plenty to do to prepare for this joint venture."

Though it was night, and we needed to refresh our bodies and minds for the next day, most of us felt a burst of energy running through our brains. We were excited about working with a large Jewish force and being able to kill two birds with one stone: attain the supplies we desperately needed while striking a vengeful blow against the German beasts. It was hard to sleep that night.

Planning The Raid

The next day, early in the morning, our small band of partisans met up with the much larger Twerskis' group. Together, we were about 100 partisans. They were just as scruffy as we were but appeared to have more weapons. The group consisted of communists, Zionists, and escaped ghetto fighters. We greeted their leader, Daniel, and his chief assistant, Mischa. We had enjoyed planning together with them for this attack and now were glad to see one another. For many of our group, this was the first meeting between the two groups. I was pleased to see that there were approximately 30 girls between both camps. Our leaders met with their leaders for most of the morning, formulating and working out the details of a plan to attack the depot.

Afterward, Daniel and Schmuel called a general meeting of all partisans.

Daniel stood before us with Schmuel at his side. Both looked quite buoyant. "We have a plan!" Daniel announced triumphantly.

The full group of attackers fell into an eerie hush, ready to absorb and memorize every spoken word. Daniel was a big man with a powerful personality that commanded attention. His baritone voice carried forcefully in the quiet of the forest clearing as he addressed us. "There is a German supply depot that has been established near a small village close to us. We've been watching them construct their barracks and lay out their minefields. They have two watchtowers and rolled barbed wire running all the way around the depot. There are a few buildings that house about 90 soldiers and their supplies, as well as office barracks and dining barracks. They also have a parking area for their trucks, motorcycles, and troop carriers."

The Twerski group looked at one another with knowing smiles. They were experienced in this sort of activity. Meanwhile, our group tried to look professionally serious, but couldn't resist breaking into delighted smiles when it slowly dawned on us as to why the parking lot was such a great target. Aha! Keeping all the vehicles in a single area made their destruction so much easier.

Daniel went on. "On scheduled days, a small military convoy of trucks enters the facility in the evening either to bring supplies to the depot or to pick them up. This coming Monday, there will be about six trucks making a delivery. At the front and back of the convoy, there will be a sidecar motorcycle, each with a driver and guard. Every truck will have a driver and a guard with a machine gun. The convoy will be made up of only soldiers. I say "soldiers," but they're really old men and young boys in uniforms. The Germans are using their best fighters at the front and mostly use old men and kids with very little military training to maintain this depot."

A derisive chuckle ran through our group.

"But, have no doubt. They can still shoot and take lives."

We became quiet.

"We have some stolen German uniforms and a captured German half-track troop carrier that we'll put to good use. We've chosen a part of the road that is closely bordered by a thick forest, with overgrown shrubs, and plants. It's only about two kilometers from the depot. We will create a distraction there that will force the convoy to stop. Our men, dressed in German uniforms, will be there, directing a group of partisans dressed as farmers. They'll be trying to remove a fallen tree off the road that we purposely put there. We'll make friendly contact with the convoy, get them to relax and even help with removing the tree. Our fake German officers speak flawless German, without an accent. A few of them will outrank anyone in the convoy. Then, we'll surprise and disarm the real Germans. We'll have partisans hidden on both sides of the road, the full length of the convoy, who will wait for the signal and then we'll strike quickly. With fast, overwhelming force, there won't be a shot fired." Daniel paused. "Well, there *shouldn't* be a shot fired."

Heads nodded enthusiastically; glowing smiles showed excitement.

"We'll replace the Germans on the convoy with our own people and put enough partisans in each truck to get the job done. Each vehicle will have a team of partisans with a specific task to accomplish. Once we get inside the depot, we'll move quickly to destroy whatever personnel are there, set our explosives, take whatever we need, and get out fast. I've chosen squad leaders who will put their teams together and go over the plan in detail with each team." Daniel scanned the sea of eager faces before him. "God be with us."

"God be with us!" the response thundered in the forest.

Daniel smiled, turned, and walked away, leaving a flurry of buzzing conversations behind him.

The weekend was full of quiet activity. Senior members of the raid went through the plan, discussing any and all contingencies, all possible variations that would require a smart and decisive response. Each participant went over his or her part again and again. Weapons were cleaned, checked and cleaned again. Monday couldn't come soon enough.

The Raid

No one had to be awakened Monday morning. As the sun came up, the camp was already abuzz. Everyone had a job to do. Proper timing would be crucial. We had to arrive at the site of the raid just early enough for the partisans to create their hiding places behind the tree line of the forest and fell a tree to block the road about five minutes before the convoy arrived. Even though this narrow road was fairly untraveled, we wanted to avoid having to deal with any other vehicles coming to this site that would create a problem for us. Blocking the road too early could complicate the plan.

We brought along a horse-drawn farm wagon as a prop, so it appeared to be a vehicle stopped by the fallen tree. The wagon was to look like it was taking workers from one farm location to another, which allowed us to have a number of supposed peasants at the scene. We then would park the half-track German troop carrier on the side of the road, while 60 partisans entered the forest and chose hiding places among the trees, shrubs, and bushes on both sides, just behind the tree line.

The Twerskis' group of partisans—dressed like a German colonel, a captain, a lieutenant, and ten soldiers—were armed with machine guns. Each of our soldiers wore a white armband imprinted with an iron cross, the letter "W", and Roman numeral "X." If the armbands prompted anyone to ask what they were about, we would say that this was a new designation for transportation soldiers. It stood for Wehrmacht, tenth group. Wehrmacht was the name for the German army. The white armbands were for our own purpose. They assured that when the firefight broke out once we were at the depot, our partisans would know who to avoid shooting. But now we had to set up.

At the appropriate time, a small explosive charge finished off the last bit of the trunk of the tree that we had prepared for easy felling. With a crash of its branches, it came to a rest, blocking the road perfectly. As soon as it dropped, the partisans in the roadside forest blended into their hiding places. They disappeared as if they were never there. It was so sudden that it felt like a visual illusion. The forest looked peaceful, quiet, even tranquil.

Partisans pushed the horse-drawn wagon up to the fallen tree and parked the German troop carrier right behind it. Our crew of actors ran to their designated places. They put ropes around the tree in two places, with some of our peasants holding each rope. A few of our soldiers stood around them, shouting orders. Other soldiers either stood around or sat on the edge of the carrier, some with bottles of wine, some with sausage and cheese. The scene was set.

The next eight minutes felt like an hour. Suddenly, we heard the sound of vehicles, at first very softly, then louder and louder until we saw the convoy approaching. The lead sidecar motorcycle sped up to reach us more quickly. It stopped behind the troop carrier. The driver and guard watched the scene for a moment, as our actors played their roles. Our soldiers shouted at our peasants to put their backs into it and hurry up.

"What is this?" the sidecar motorcycle driver asked.

Though most of the convoys were manned by older men and young boys, there were always a few real soldiers in the mix. This was one of them.

"This tree decided to take a nap in the road," our soldier answered. "We're trying to get these stupid Polish peasants to move it, but I think it's too much for them."

At that point our partisan dressed as a colonel strode up. "We may need your help to move it."

"Yes, Colonel," the driver snapped, obeying rank.

"But first let's have some good wine, sausage, and a little cheese. A quick bite and we'll have the energy to move a mountain, eh?"

The driver, guard, and our colonel shared a laugh. Then, the colonel made a hand signal, and our soldiers brought the food and drink forward. They began to distribute it among the trucks. The drivers and guards met our soldiers with welcoming conversation, leaned their weapons against the trucks and began sharing the food and wine. The driver and guard from the rear motorcycle walked up to the middle of the convoy to join their comrades in conversation and a welcomed snack. As soon as the Germans became relaxed, our colonel turned to the convoy members. "I have something important to tell you all!" he shouted, loudly enough to be heard by the convoy. "I wish you all a good life. So here is a toast." He raised his glass, as did all the German soldiers with a drink in their hand. "Do not move!" our colonel continued sternly.

The convoy personnel looked puzzled.

At that moment our soldiers pointed their machine guns at the convoy members and loudly repeated, "Do not move, or you die!"

Suddenly the trees and brush exploded with armed partisans who aimed their guns at the shocked Germans. "Do not move! Raise your hands!" they shouted as they quickly covered the few feet before them to present a deadly force surrounding the German soldiers.

As expected, and hoped for, the real Germans froze in place, terrified, their hands full with wine and food instead of weapons. Part one of the plan worked out perfectly.

As the Germans were bound and gagged, our peasants and soldiers threw chains around the tree, attached them to the troop carrier and dragged the tree until it was parallel to the road. The partisans then rearranged the freight in the trucks to make room for each team of fighters, about ten in each vehicle. Our soldiers quickly looked over the papers of the convoy members to make sure there would be no surprises if we were asked questions at the depot gate. Satisfied that all was in order, our soldiers manned the trucks and got into the troop carrier. The partisans dressed as peasants took their place in the horse-drawn wagon and started off along the road toward the depot. The plan was for our convoy to overtake the wagon about half a kilometer before the depot, so that while the convoy entered the facility, the wagon would arrive close enough to provide extra support.

Everything went incredibly smooth. Our convoy waited until the horse-drawn wagon got closer to the depot. Then, they surged forward. As planned, the convoy passed the horse-drawn wagon and went on to the main gate of the depot. The first truck, with our colonel aboard, stayed close to the lead motorcycle, so the rank of our officer would prevail over any suspicions or difficult questions.

Our motorcycle came to a halt at the gate as the first truck pulled up behind. Our colonel immediately got out, surprising the guards with his rank. They weren't used to seeing high-ranking officers on these convoys. Both gate guards snapped to attention as the German inside the gatehouse, almost comically, sprang to attention like a jack-in-the-box.

Our colonel answered their salute with a short *Heil Hitler* gesture. Then, before being asked, he thrust the appropriate documents forward to one of the guards.

"It's been a long, boring journey," our colonel said. "We are tired and hungry. We wish to get on with our delivery. Do you understand?" he told the guards in a serious tone.

The message was clear.

"*Jawohl!*"

As hoped, the guard only skimmed through the papers, barely reading the words. He handed them back to our colonel and said, "Everything is in order. You may proceed."

Our colonel smiled, took the papers back and said to the soldier, "I have been told this is a very efficient group here. I can see this is true."

The soldier, holding back a smile of gratitude and relief, clicked his heels together and gave a quick military nod. He then added, "Herr Colonel, if you and your men are hungry, you may want to have something to eat at the dining hall. It is mealtime now."

"Good!" our colonel replied. He turned and motioned the convoy to move forward as the second guard lifted the gate.

At that moment the horse-drawn wagon approached the rear of our convoy. The guards turned their heads toward the wagon, now able to take their eyes off our colonel.

"What is this?" one guard asked the other, unshouldering his weapon.

"Oh," our colonel said, "we told a wagon of Polish peasants to follow us and help with loading our materials. Why waste good free labor, eh?"

"Ah," the guard said. "Yes, perhaps they're good for something after all."

Our colonel smiled at him. He was reassured enough to put the butt of his machine gun on the ground. "We'll drive to the storage barracks then," our colonel said, "but first we'll get something to eat at the dinner barracks. Can one of you direct us to these places?"

The guard who had examined the papers motioned to the second guard to lead the convoy. "Gruber will direct you."

Gruber, a wide-eyed teenage soldier, ran to the front of the convoy, turned and faced it, then shouted and pointed directions to both places. Our colonel got back into the truck and gestured to the driver to enter the gate. The convoy followed, except for the rear motorcycle and guard, who remained at the gate, telling the guards they'd escort the peasants to where they had to unload the materials. They engaged the guards in conversation while the horse-drawn wagon pulled up to the gate.

The trucks moved through the camp, spreading out in different directions as they moved deeper into the depot. Being dinner time, with most of the compound's soldiers in the dining hall, the trucks raised no suspicion on the premises. It was normal for traffic to move about the camp once past the security of the main gate. Two trucks drove to opposite sides of the dinner barracks and parked. Partisans disguised as German soldiers exited the trucks and took their positions, covering all exits of the dinner barracks. The other four trucks drove to a clear site line of the four guard towers. The fifth guard tower, at the main gate, was easily covered by our sidecar motorcycle driver and guard, and the horse-drawn wagon team. Two of our German soldiers had gotten into position at the communications section of the main depot office. Their task involved putting explosives in place and setting them off at the agreed-upon signal so all communication to the outside world would be blocked.

Now, timing was of utmost importance. The smallest delay in action by any of the teams could result in the loss of surprise and, consequently, the loss of many precious lives. The partisans had thought out the starting signal carefully.

Suddenly, a startlingly bright light lit up the night. Partisans had sent up a flare, lighting up the dusk sky. Action and noise exploded simultaneously. Machine gun fire erupted from the trucks in long blinding bursts, aimed at the guard towers. Every tower exploded from the sheer volume of firepower. Pieces of wood filled the air like confetti. The Tower Guards, having no chance to return fire, became human fragments.

The motorcycle team, together with the horse-drawn wagon team, cut down the gate guards and main tower in an instant. Then, the horse-drawn wagon team spread out in a half circle about 30 meters away from the main gate. Heavy machine guns were trained on the narrow opening. While the barbed wire of the camp had been designed to keep unwanted intruders out of the depot, it also allowed no one to leave it. The gate was the only exit from the compound, and the horse-drawn wagon team had it covered.

At the sleeping barracks, partisans ran into the building and shot anything and everything. Outside the dinner barracks, machine gun fire, tank bazookas, and hand grenades raked and destroyed every inch of the building. As expected, many German soldiers inside the barracks dropped to the ground to avoid the gunfire, while others ran to the exits in an attempt to escape.

After the initial salvo of weapons and explosives, only a few of the soldiers inside the dining hall remained alive. Those reaching the exits were strafed into pieces as they came through the doorway. When the first roar of gunfire dimmed, partisans ran to the windows and strafed the floor in a broom-sweeping pattern to finish off any possibility of a threat. Actually, that was overkill, because the building was now a roaring bonfire filled with lethal smoke.

In the first minute of the firefight, partisans poured out of the trucks and ran through the camp to eliminate any stragglers. Sounds of shooting erupted in bursts all over the camp, lasting only about 30 seconds in each location. Some German soldiers were scattered around the depot, who had been lounging back at the barracks, taking care of business at the office, in the motor pool, or in transit from one part of the depot to another. They, like most soldiers, were trained to always have their weapon at hand, so we knew we couldn't completely avoid return fire. However, none of the firefights lasted more than a couple of minutes. A few of the Germans immediately understood the overwhelming odds against them and dropped their weapons, raised their hands in the air, and shouted in German and broken Polish that they surrendered. We didn't have the luxury of time or humanity and gunned them down. We had no way to take care of prisoners and we couldn't leave them. They might identify us or come back as soldiers to hunt us down and kill us. Most of the partisans would endure endless nights of fitful sleep over this necessary decision.

The element of surprise and the overwhelming firepower had accomplished more than the partisans could have imagined. Even with that, five partisans were killed and at least 15 wounded by enemy or friendly fire. Such were the tragic consequences of warfare.

As teams of partisans swept the entire compound looking for stragglers, the rest of us went to work in the supply buildings, culling out weapons, ammunition, medical supplies, food, and clothing that we desperately needed. The women were charged with helping to find supplies, choose which ones to leave and which to take, and organize the loading of them. Oddly, we had no fear. The chaos of the firefights, and doing our designated tasks kept us too busy to worry about being shot. Two teams quickly checked the cargo already on the truck to see if any of it served our needs. The trucks were then loaded with the supplies while three demolition teams set charges throughout the depot. Initially, we only had enough charges to blow up a few things, but we discovered a large cache of explosives in one building and expanded our demolition capability fourfold.

We laughed at the irony of blowing up the German depot with its own explosives. The charges were set on timers, which allowed us to get a safe distance away before they went off. We started the engines of the trucks, finally filled with our future, and drove them out the main gate, which was now a smoldering pile of embers.

When we'd gone a few kilometers down the road, the darkening night sky suddenly lit up with a thousand flares. We looked back with joy to see and hear the depot exploding into nothingness. Some of us counted aloud, from the first light of the explosives until the sound of the blasts caught up to us.

"Ha! That's four kilometers away," Schmuel announced, remembering how to count the time between a lightning strike and the sound of thunder that follows it to determine how far away the strike happened.

A roar went up from the partisans. How sweet was the taste of revenge!

As the trucks rolled on to our agreed upon meeting place, we fell into silence, each mulling over the raid in his or her own way. No one spoke. We just moved. The raid was over and we needed to get back to the forest to hide and disperse our goods, and to prepare for the inevitable reprisal from the Germans. We were ready. We had fought proudly as Jews and struck a blow against the German war machine. An intoxicating sense of pride filled our hearts.

After the Raid

When we arrived at the pre-arranged locale in the forest, our comrades and members of the Twerski partisans who stayed behind warmly greeted us. We were immediately bombarded with questions about the raid, eager ears wanting to hear every detail of it. After a quick meal, during which we told those left behind about our adventure, item-by-item and minute-by-minute, we divided up the various supplies between our group and that of the Twerskis. The division was fair, giving shares according to the number of people in each group. When it was over, our share didn't look as bountiful as we'd thought, but that was okay. The important thing was that the mission was successful because of the cooperative effort of two Jewish fighting groups. We felt that we'd not only answered a need but did it in cooperation with some of our own people.

I was especially thankful for the medicines we captured. We had previously had a bout of typhus from our lice infestation and those who caught it were terribly sick.

Once the trucks were emptied, the boys drove them a short distance into the forest and covered them with branches and shrubs, so they were not easily visible. Then they did their best to cover their truck tracks, using branches as makeshift brooms. They also sprinkled stones and leaves, just enough to blend in with the surroundings. Schmuel and Sol had already decided to hide most of the things we captured in some caves they had discovered weeks before the raid. After covering up our traces, we warmly said our goodbyes to the Twerskis and the other Jewish partisans. They were no longer just Jews or fellow fighters. Now, they were family.

On our way back to camp, I heard Schmuel and Meir talking. Schmuel was asking if Meir had noticed the age of most of the German soldiers. He nodded.

"It was hard not to notice that they were mostly older men and young boys. The Germans must be running out of regular soldiers. I hope so."

"Well," Schmuel began, "I can tell you I'm feeling great about the supplies we captured, but I am feeling even better about the damage we did to a German army unit. Just think about all the horrendous things we've seen these pigs do." He stopped and spit three times, a superstitious belief to ward off evil. "We hear about what the Germans are doing to our relatives, friends and any Jew they can torture or brutalize. Well, it gives me satisfaction to deal them a harsh blow of vengeance and justice."

"*Omayn*," Meir replied, voicing his blessing. "Actually, I hate to be a hater. It's sick. I will be glad when this is over. I hope we have family left that will survive this nightmare."

With that, the brothers embraced and fell into silence as we made our way deeper into the forest.

In the Forest

The next few months were filled with healing and activity. We took some precious time off to rest. Sufficient medication and adequate clothing, along with fresh warm food, energized our bodies as well as our spirits. As our health improved, the group became eager to attack the Germans again, to taste the joys of victory and revenge as we had in the raid on the depot.

Two unexpected events would sharply define what the next step had to be. One day Noah Orbach, one of our defensive guards, approached Schmuel with a serious look on his face. Noah was in charge of perimeter security. He knew the forest as if he'd grown it himself and his senses were as keen as an animal's. Schmuel trusted his judgment and instincts without question.

"I think we are being followed," Noah said in a guarded tone.

"Why do you say that?" Schmuel asked, sensing the gravity of concern in his voice.

"I don't know, but looking out into the forest, things just don't seem right. Something is out of place."

"Thanks, Noah. We'll investigate it immediately."

If this report had come from anyone else, Schmuel might have waved it off. Coming from Noah, it had to be acted upon immediately. So Schmuel called a meeting with Sol and Meir. They discussed the problem, and mutually decided to get their best group of fighters together and investigate the locale that Noah had pointed out as being suspicious. They put together a forward team of scouts, supported by an even bigger backup team of fighters. I was allowed to come along.

The forward scout team consisted of six partisans working in pairs, one of those pairs being Schmuel and Noah. They moved quickly and quietly from tree to tree and rock to rock, each pair of scouts carefully leapfrogging the pair ahead of them, quietly investigating each zone as they moved forward. There didn't seem to be any basis for Noah's fear, other than his incredible instincts. Then, suddenly, one of the men in the front held up his hand quickly and everyone froze. Schmuel and Noah quietly moved up to him. The fighter pointed to his own ear and then to the forest before him—a signal to listen carefully. Schmuel heard some sounds that were hard to describe. He waved the group to move forward stealthily. As they advanced, they heard soft voices and the sounds of movement, getting louder and louder with their approach. Schmuel signaled the other two pairs to stop while he and Noah advanced slowly and carefully, moving across the forest floor with surprising stealth. Now with the voices and sounds at their loudest, they froze in place, to listen more carefully.

Before them they saw 11 people sitting around two small fires, warming themselves and chatting as if they were in no danger. Schmuel signaled Noah to go back and return with the rest of the partisan fighters, adding a sign that meant we should surround the target group and await his signal to close in quickly. Noah nodded, turned, and disappeared. Schmuel waited patiently, observing the actions of the group around the campfires. The partisan fighters broke up into teams of three, then moved up silently to surround the small camp. When everyone was in place, Schmuel signaled to those who could see him to move into action. Those who couldn't see him, would follow the flow of activity when the group moved in. I was part of that group.

As soon as the first partisans sprang forward, the rest of us followed, surprising the startled group around the fires. To the shock of Schmuel and his friends, the group, standing with their hands in the air, were mostly teenagers who looked no older than 16 or 17 years old. Their clothes were tattered rags and the few weapons they had looked old and poorly maintained. Their meager supplies were carelessly scattered about. Schmuel counted eight boys and three girls comprising the group, guessing the youngest to be about ten years old. He loudly demanded, "Who are you? What are you doing here?"

One of the boys took a careful step forward and, with his hands raised, managed to point at himself. "My name is Yonathon Boyarski. They call me Yoni. Most of us are from the village of Dabrowice. As far as we know, we are all that remains of our families. What you see here is a group of Jewish fighters. We are looking for a group of Jewish partisans called the The Foxes of Parczew."

Schmuel and the fighters chuckled. He thought to himself how amateur and careless this child was to admit being a Jewish partisan to a group he didn't know. Admitting to being any kind of a Jew, partisan or not, without knowing for sure who you were addressing, was dangerous business. Still, he liked the fearless, almost careless, nature of this thin, dark-haired boy.

"The Parczew Foxes?" Schmuel repeated in a mocking musical tone. "Hmm, I like it." He and the rest of us looked at one another with amused smiles. "I think you have found who you are looking for. I must say that your security is very poor, but luckily it was *us* who found *you*."

"Yes, that was our plan. You Foxes are too clever to be found, so we hoped you would find us. We thought that if we made enough noise, that might happen. It looks like it did."

Schmuel smiled and thought, *Ha! Who's the fox now?*

"Tell me," he asked, "As fighters, what have you achieved?"

Yoni's dark, piercing eyes darted from man to man, studying the faces of Schmuel and his group, as he carefully decided what to answer. The teen took a breath and said, "Last week we burned down an important wooden bridge over a deep gorge that the Germans were using to transport materials and soldiers."

The "Parczew Foxes" glanced at one another, delightful surprise on our faces. *Children did this?*

"Why did you choose that target? How did you know it was important?"

Joni dropped his hands, using them to emphasize his enthusiastic explanation. "Well, we watched that bridge for a week, keeping track of the number of vehicles that went back and forth, and it was obvious that if the bridge was gone, the Germans would have no other way to get over the gorge." He paused for a moment, pleased by the positive reaction he read on the faces of our group, encouraged by our full attention. "So, we went into town and asked the local people to give us some kerosene. Unbelievably, they refused. We pleaded with them, but they still told us no. I think they were either afraid of the Germans finding out that they helped us, or they saw a bunch of raggedy children and didn't take us seriously. We knew that if we didn't act fast, they might turn us in, so we pointed our guns at them and made it very clear to the villagers that if they didn't help us, we would help ourselves—over their dead bodies. They immediately cooperated. We got the kerosene we needed and even a little food. We let them know that if any Germans came after us, we'd assume they'd turned us in and we'd come back and burn the village to the ground. They decided to cooperate and live. We waited until early in the morning, just before the change of guards, when there were the fewest soldiers, and they'd be tired from a long night on duty. We shot all four of the guards before they could call for help. Then we set the bridge on fire and escaped. It is probably still smoking. It was a great fire."

"So, what now?" Schmuel asked, trying to hide his admiration for this band of ragtags.

"We don't know. Look at us. We don't have enough supplies to sustain ourselves. Or to make war. There are more bridges to burn down, more Germans to shoot. We need your help. We want to join you."

Schmuel became quiet, stroking his chin in thought as he took a poll of our faces, measuring our looks of empathy and admiration for these young fighters. "Yonathon, Jews don't turn away Jews. Follow us."

We Need Supplies

The sounds of the forest surrounded our most recent camp. Every so often, the entire group would relocate, after removing all traces of our presence at the previous camp and the journey to the present one. Here, deep in the forest, there wasn't a hint that a war was raging somewhere around them. The tranquility of this camp could tempt the most warlike of the group to lie back and relax.

In the glow of the setting sun filtering through the trees, we just finished dinner. Schmuel, Sol, and Meir had been joined by Sasha Skolnik and Joel Zigman, valuable veteran fighters, who came to report on the latest group to join "The Foxes," as we now called themselves.

"So?" Schmuel asked Sasha, "How are the new fighters doing?"

"We gave the kids a good meal, clothes, and weapons. They feel like they found heaven, even though it was us who found them wandering in the forest," he replied, peering over his reading glasses at Schmuel. This quiet-mannered mouse of a man had been an accountant in a small village. He loved his peaceful world of numbers. Then, German atrocities against the Jews, especially women and children, had turned him into a deadly, vengeful animal.

"There's more," Sasha added.

"More what?"

"We found two families lost in the woods. How's that for a coincidence? First, we find the kids, then we find the families. This is getting to be a crowded neighborhood."

Schmuel chuckled. "Tell me about them? Where are they from?"

"There are two families. They escaped from the Lodz Ghetto."

"That's a bad one," Schmuel groaned. "How many are there?"

"Ben Moskovitz and his family are five and Viktor Sirkin and his family are another four, a total of nine additional people to our group. It's hard to believe, but these two families escaped through the sewers, wading and swimming through unthinkable filth. Ben almost drowned. They found their way to us with the help of some friendly Polish villagers. They were filthy from the sewers and totally exhausted. It's a miracle that both families survived. These people will be a positive addition to the camp. They're ready to do anything we ask them to do. Their children are young and refreshing to have around."

Schmuel turned to us. "We are so lucky, my friends, that so many of us are still alive, even though the Germans have tried otherwise. Now, according to everything we hear, the war seems to be approaching its end, but we have growing problems that must be dealt with if we are to survive."

Everyone's eyes and ears were locked on Schmuel.

"Sasha, when I asked you to give me an inventory of our supplies a week ago, you told me we were running low on many things. How bad is our situation?"

"All of our supplies *are* running low and decreasing rapidly," Sasha answered. "Our ammunition and explosives are down because we have used them on our constant raids to destroy enemy telephone lines and communications. We've ambushed small German troop convoys and have been in firefights, as you well know. When you add the additional mouths to feed, bodies to clothe, fighters to supply with weapons, and illnesses that must be attended to, well, we're in real trouble. The two families from the Lodz Ghetto and the children from Dabrowice alone amount to 20 more people to care for and supply. We just don't have enough. We must do something soon."

Our group became quiet, lost in thought.

"I pray every night for relief," Sasha went on. "I know that God helps those who help themselves. Well, we've been helping ourselves. So, when does God do His part?"

"Since you're on speaking terms with God, ask Him to rain down supplies on us," Schmuel quipped.

Sol raised his hand. "Wait a minute! I think God is about to do that."

Schmuel laughed. "I was being sarcastic. You're crazy."

"Not at all," Sol shot back, his energy suddenly apparent. "That's exactly what's going to happen. It's going to rain supplies. Let me explain."

The Air-Drop

"Schmuel," Sol went on, "Meir and I often talk about the lucky communist partisans who don't have to raid to get supplies. The Russian Army drops air shipments about every two weeks. We joke together about them not missing a few cases of supplies if we were clever enough to steal them. For us, it was only a joke."

"And now, maybe it's a plan?" Meir suggested.

Schmuel's eyes narrowed, and a mischievous smile slowly grew. "I believe we have a plan right from the heavens. God *is* doing His part."

Excited ideas shot back and forth among the group and the plan came together in just a few minutes.

Schmuel gathered the planning committee of the Foxes of Parczew together and suggested the strategy. He started with the obvious downside: The very idea of stealing from the communist partisans involved enormous risk. Immediately, many of the partisans shook their heads and frowned at one another. In no way could The Foxes be completely invisible. The communists would have their own people at the drop zone to quickly retrieve the supplies, so they'd see The Foxes when we showed up. Since the drop always took place in a meadow that was closer to their base than the Fox camp, they could marshal more fighters quickly if they needed reinforcements. However, to The Foxes' advantage, we usually only sent out just enough people to collect the materials. Also, these supplies were not a matter of life or death for the communists, since they received regular drops and even had a surplus. They just weren't worth dying for. The Foxes, on the other hand, were desperate. For us, it would mean death if we didn't get them soon.

It was helpful that Schmuel had already met the leader of the communists, Sergei Rubinov, and had even asked him for supplies, which he refused. Schmuel knew that Sergei had a reputation for never trusting anyone else to do a job right, so he showed up at every activity of his group. He'd certainly be at the drop.

The plan required putting its elements in place days before the drop, before the communists came to the meadow. Schmuel put Meir in charge of selecting and assigning the backup men. They decided to bring a good-sized force, at least larger than the communists, to the drop zone. Meir would take a backup force of 20 partisans and hide in the tall grass and trees around the edge of the meadow, while Schmuel would lead a force of 12 to collect the packages. Schmuel's presence would be important If Sergei showed up at the meadow. since he would need to see a familiar face quickly to avoid an unfortunate clash. A scout team of four men would watch the communist camp situated at the far end of the meadow, and radio the information back to Meir and Schmuel through stolen German field phones.

Sol knew where to steal a truck to haul whatever we could pick up. If they used our own truck—which they had hidden in the forest —the chance of being spotted on the journey to the drop site was too great. A stolen truck was much safer. Once the drop took place, the Foxes would have to take whatever we could get their hands on and leave in a hurry. They didn't think they'd have time to grab more than could fit in the vehicle.

The Foxes found two locations where we could hide the supplies quickly. We would come back to retrieve them later, when it was safe. We figured we should be able to get some of the parcels before the communist partisans appeared. If and when the communists showed up, Schmuel would try to reason with Sergei and hope for the best.

Plan in Action

Two days before the scheduled time of the raid, thirty-three Parczew Foxes set out through the forest for the site of the air-drop: a large meadow surrounded by tall grass and trees. It took about three to four hours to walk the ten-kilometer distance. Once there, We cautiously moved within sight of the communist camp, about a half a kilometer beyond the far end of the meadow. We then settled into the adjacent forest. We had come early enough to avoid missing the drop and needed to remain hidden.

The first day passed with weather so stormy, the Russians wouldn't fly in it. On the second day of waiting and watching, the distant sound of airplane engines told us that the game was finally on. The scout team watching the communist camp, saw a small group getting horses and wagons ready to go to the drop zone. They kept their eyes on both the sky and the camp, using the stolen German field phones to report everything they saw. Schmuel's group of 12 partisans, including me, stood at the tree line adjacent to the edge of the meadow, farthest from the communist camp. Meir's team of 18 fighters spread out in the tall grass and lay down flat on the ground, virtually disappearing from sight. Everyone watched the sky intensely, waiting for the airplanes appeared.

The distant sound of roaring engines up high told the group that the drop was getting close. As the planes approached the meadow, their doors opened and packages fell out, trailed by light green chutes that looked like tubes until they suddenly popped open into full, air-filled chutes and started floating downward. Upon seeing the cargo planes, Schmuel's group ran to the fringe of the meadow, and waited until the packages hit the ground, one after another. Then, we ran out, grabbed the packages closest to us and threw them onto the truck that Sol had driven into the meadow from its hiding place in the forest. From the other end of the meadow, communist partisans appeared with horses and wagons, lumbering toward the packages. Galloping out front, on a sleek, brown horse Sergei led a group of communists to the meadow. As they got closer and saw The Foxes, they picked up their pace. Sergei began screaming something at the top of his lungs. Schmuel told us to keep moving. Sergei pulled his horse up in front of Schmuel and quickly dismounted.

"What's going on here?" he demanded while his men gathered around Schmuel, their rifles at the ready.

"Sergei!" Schmuel greeted the angry communist with a bright, friendly voice. The Foxes kept their weapons shouldered, so they wouldn't be seen as a threat. "I have to be honest. We need supplies. We're fighting Germans just like you. We're in this together. We should be helping each other. The more of us doing this, the sooner this war is over, but we're out of supplies. We'll die without them." His gaze locked hard onto Sergei's angry eyes.

"They are ours!" Sergei growled, his men anxiously fingering their weapons.

Schmuel's voice was calm, even soft; his demeanor, friendly. "Sergei, I have a large force here, but I don't want to get into a fight. We both need our energy and resources to use against the damned Nazis. I'll tell you what. We will take what we already have and get out of your area. I will take all my people with me."

Schmuel made a hand signal and six men, with their weapons in plain view, stood up from their hiding places in the tall grass as if they grew straight from the ground. Sergei looked sarcastically amused at this so-called "large force."

Schmuel went on. "Comrade, there are still several bundles in the meadow, and we know you will get another drop in a couple of weeks. If I get any good information, I promise to pass it on to you." He made another hand gesture and six more fighters stood. Then six more, each of them with weapons in hand, though not pointed at the communists.

Sergei saw the value of cooling down, though he was still angry. Now, the 12 of us who had just finished loading the truck trotted back to stand behind Schmuel. Sergei nodded to his own men with an unforgettable menacing glare, and they lowered their weapons, obeying his body language.

He looked at Schmuel, took a deep breath, forced a smile and said, "I want to support you, comrade, but don't do this again. We are on the same side and stealing from each other does not sit well."

Schmuel held out his hand, inviting a handshake, which Sergei took reluctantly and muttered, "Thank you, comrade."

As The Foxes left the meadow, Schmuel could hear Sergei talking to his men. He could understand some Russian and was relieved to hear Sergei instructing his soldiers to stand down and relax. Meir's ruse had worked so far. The Foxes picked up our pace and made it to the truck, where a smiling Sol was waiting.

Schmuel shouted, "Go, Sol, go! Let's get out of here!"

The truck drove off with its prized cargo, followed by The Parczew Foxes.

We would receive a hero's welcome back at camp.

The War Ends

On May 7, 1945, Colonel General Alfred Jodl signed an instrument of unconditional surrender to the Allies. The Americans, British, Russians, and French partisans, as well as the partisan armies from other European countries, had done their part to finally force the German war machine into submission. Sadly, the cost was incredible. Six million Jews were dead, as well as countless millions of innocents.

The news of the surrender was slow to reach many of the partisan armies. Deep in the Parczew forest in Poland, we received the news with joy, but also with restrained celebration. We had endured starvation, disease, and sickness with the knowledge that our loved ones either had been or were being exterminated. Some members of The Foxes had survived the suffering in the ghetto, others had escaped from death camps. They had fought with every possible tool and weapon in their possession and in every way they could to hit back at the Nazis. Our group, in spite of the Polish animosity toward us and receiving little or no help from the Polish population, still focused on our mission to do what we could to make things as difficult as possible for the Germans. Now it was over. And the oppressed had prevailed.

Schmuel and Sol called the entire group of The Parczew Foxes together. Schmuel stood before them, addressing them with emotion in his voice. "My fellow comrades, the war is finally over. We have done the best we could to fight the Germans. As Jews, we should always be proud that we fought back and were actually effective. Now the time has come for us to go our own ways. We all have decisions to make about our futures. There are options available. Palestine awaits those who can get there. Countries like the United States, Great Britain, Australia, South Africa, even South America, are also possibilities, in spite of the quotas. Speaking for myself, I have no desire to remain in Poland, the land of my birth."

He took a deep breath and, looking over the group, continued. "Antisemitism still breeds here. I wish to go to a place where I can raise a family that will have the opportunity to live freely and make of themselves what they can. I want my family to embrace the Jewish values my parents and grandparents taught me. Those are my goals."

He hesitated a moment and scanned the faces of his fellow partisans with whom he had shared so many trials and adventures. We looked at him with tears in our eyes, frozen in the moment. With a sigh, he continued. "I will never forget all of you and the experiences we have shared. I hope you will all be secure in your futures. I pray that each and every one of you are able to find living members of your family who have survived the Nazi genocide. May God bless us all."

With that sobering speech, the meeting broke up. Just like that. Little groups formed to say their goodbyes and to discuss their possible futures. The morning would bring new beginnings, new adventures. I was ready for that.

8

AVRUM
APRIL 1945 TO OCTOBER 1945

Liberation

By the spring of 1945, the war that seemed endless showed hopeful signs of finally ending. In its wake, it left tragedy and desolation. Millions of Jews in concentration camps had died, with a final tally of deaths that would shock history forever. At Dachau, we noticed subtle changes. There were fewer German SS troops around, and the camp regularly received more conscripted German Army soldiers to replace the feared storm troopers. Still, we were kept working, with inmates dying all around us.

The ovens burned 24 hours a day, but still couldn't keep up the death rate expected by Hitler. Bodies designated to become ashes were, instead, piled high in large mass graves dug out by bulldozers. Some were left in the open to rot. Generous portions of lye were thrown on the piles of humanity, but that only slowed down the process of returning to the soil. We had been receiving inmates from other camps who arrived by what they called "death marches." So many started the journey, and so few finished.

On April 29, the US Seventh Army's 45th infantry division showed up at our gates. Our camp, Dachau, was the first camp established by Hitler, and now, coincidentally, the first camp liberated by the

Americans. It had been an important camp for producing armaments and training SS soldiers. The Americans arrived at the gates in a strangely quiet manner, without advanced explosives or a firefight. The Germans understood that the war was really over and were prepared to surrender. There were journalists present when the camp was handed over by an SS officer to a commanding officer of the United States Army. While this was going on, the American soldiers just outside the gate discovered a train of over 30 rail cars filled with decomposing bodies. The scene of all those dead men, women, and children violated all the rules of human decency. The stench was awful.

The Americans were appalled at what they saw and smelled. They flew into an uncontrolled rage, furious at this brutal and disgusting sight. We heard gunshots from the infuriated US soldiers and the voices of Germans pleading for their lives. Some prisoners got their hands on guns and set out on a killing spree. Inmates used anything they could find as a weapon to exact revenge on the Germans. The Americans did nothing to stop them.

I stood in the yard with my friend, Ezra, watching and trying to understand everything happening around us. Most of the inmate laborers had remained quiet until they understood the reality of what was taking place. Then, their joy erupted. In their pitiful condition, they tried to hug the Americans who, on the other hand, avoided *being* hugged because so many of the inmates were covered with scabs and lice.

Gradually, the US Army got everything organized and called up their medical units on the double. Many of us stood back, out of harm's way, and just followed the flow of what was going on. We were spectators to history. I felt unexpected emotions: joy, disgust, fulfillment, anger, empathy, and confusion. My elation was subdued even though I was quite happy. Surprisingly, my priorities turned to the simplest and most pressing of needs: hunger. My mind listened to my stomach, which said I needed to eat. But where was the food? Most prisoners were warned not to eat handouts from the soldiers. We were told that it could cause us harm. *How could food cause harm?* Sadly, many did not listen, and bodies that had managed to digest the small portions of soupy gruel we had received over the months and years could not process the nutrient-rich food of the Americans—many died. So many were already dead and now, on this eve of liberation, these poor people died as well.

The next day, the US Army forced the residents of the nearby city of Dachau to come to the death camp to view the hideous product of the German military and bury the bodies that were strewn all around. It was sad—and disgusting—that the residents said they had no idea that something like this had been going on so close by. Dachau is only 31 kilometers from Munich, Germany.

The Day After

The day after liberation, I walked outside our barracks with Ezra. We were thinking about the enormity of the war finally being over. I told him that it pleased me that we were liberated by the Americans and not the Russians or the British.

"The Russians will certainly liberate many camps—and thank God for that—but they have never been kind to the Jews. The British will also, God willing, liberate many camps, but they've never been fair to the Jews either. In fact, they block us from entering to Palestine. I am told that America, a country that is only about 150 years old, is made up of people from all over the world. They know and understand our grief. So many of them and their families have come from harsh situations in other countries. These Americans have compassion for other people. Yes, I am glad they rescued us. It is almost like the Messiah has touched us."

Ezra nodded and said, "With all our disease and sickness, and the torture we've been through, I hope they can help us heal from this oppression, not only our bodies, but also our minds, and most of all, our souls. Then, we can count our dead and say Kaddish for them."

"Yes, we will give our attention to the living and find others like us, so we can move forward. We have been chosen to survive for a reason. We can't complain about 'Why me? Why us?' We must move forward. You will find whoever of your family has been spared and I will find Lena, God willing."

Returning Home

The Americans turned the concentration camp into a DP (displaced persons) camp, with hospital facilities, a kitchen dedicated to good food, and lice-free beds. After so much death and evil, the liberated inmates of the camp were given a chance to get physically healthy and try to prepare themselves for a life to come. Mental health would be a longer process, with the possibility of failure for many.

For many, liberation came too late. Throughout the camp, there were still piles of dead bodies in pits and cremation ovens full of ashes. I was numb. I needed to gain back the feelings that were crushed by the Germans and suppressed by myself in order to survive. I looked at the people around me. They all looked alike: gaunt skeletons with sunken eyes showing no glimmer of hope. Yet, hidden in each survivor, a desire to live burned like a smoldering ember ready to catch fire. None of us could grasp the scope of what had happened.

The camp now offered a variety of different activities to keep us occupied and help us back to health. Theater and musical groups came to perform. A newspaper sprang up out of nowhere and we wallowed in the joy of being informed about everything on a daily basis. I tried to adjust to a life where real food was the norm, a life without the constant threat of sadistic *Kapos* hovering over me.

I went to the camp authorities to seek help with locating my family. They showed me a long list of names of who survived and who did not. As big as it was, and though the list helped many people, it wasn't complete. Reading through the names hit me hard. It was staggering to come to terms with the number of Jews who were gone. Parents, grandparents, siblings, and cousins—gone. Whole families were wiped out. I thought of my parents but had little hope that they survived. *What of Lena? Yes, I must get healthy and find her.*

I decided that as soon as I was able, I would go back to my hometown, the last place where I knew she had been. With the war over, I thought that people would certainly be helpful. So I prepared my mind for the task, which felt like a blessing, because it gave me a direction and a purpose. It would be a fairly long trip to Leszno, but it wouldn't be long before I was physically fit again. I looked forward to finally finding my sister.

The Mission

Day by day, I could feel my body healing. Eating healthy food on a regular basis without having to work long hours under brutal conditions allowed me to continually improve. With that improvement, I felt my mind healing as well. This new strength reinforced my determination to find my sister, Lena. I was on a mission, a quest that wouldn't be denied. I checked all the lists of survivors for Lena's name, as well as the lists of those who died. Occasionally, I ran across a name I knew from our village, but I found nothing about my relatives.

One day, as I walked to my barracks, I thought I saw someone I knew from my hometown. I pushed my way through a crowd of people until I found Symon Rosencransz, who had been two years ahead of me in school. I shouted his name. When he turned to see who was calling, his face lit up like a candle. Both thrilled to see a familiar face, we hugged one another, grinning the entire time. He told me that he was on his way to Palestine and was excited about it. He had joined a group of Polish and Russian Jews who decided they did not want to go back to their homes and thought that Palestine offered the best future. I asked about his family, who had been friends of my parents. He told me that as far as he knew, he was the only survivor. I could tell that he'd dealt with this realization for a long time, which allowed him to talk about it without emotion interfering. I told him I was looking for information about my parents and other members of my family.

He said, "I don't know about your aunts and uncles, but I must tell you, look no further for your parents. They are gone and in a better place now."

Oh? I thought to myself. *The best place for my parents is right here, alive, next to me.* But even though I had hoped that he was wrong, I was now faced with the stark reality of it. Admitting to myself that they might actually be gone was a stunning blow. Symon had lost his family and I had also lost mine. I had heard this same story many times.

"Avrum." Symon's soft voice nudged me out of my thoughts. "Maybe you would be interested in going to Palestine. What do you think?"

"I don't know. I'm sure you remember my little sister, Lena."

"Yes, I do." He sighed.

"My father, God bless him, had the foresight to hide her from the Nazis. I am not sure where she is, but I need to try to find her. I remember my father asking a Polish merchant to hide her. I can't remember his name, so much has happened. If I can find her, then I can decide where I want to go."

He nodded. "Good luck to you, Avrum."

We hugged warmly and he left to join his group headed to Palestine.

Looking for Lena

After a few months, even though I was feeling better, I wasn't as healthy as I wanted to be, or needed to be. Our displaced person's camp (DP camp) had become a swarm of liberated inmates and lost souls, not all of whom were Jews. In fact, there were even displaced Germans and Poles in the camp, most of them hostile to Jews. Some had supervised Jewish labor on many levels and had been in a superior position to the Jewish labor force. Since we remained in what had once been a concentration camp, we still had barbed wire surrounding us, a reminder of a tortured past. I don't know why the Americans didn't take the time to remove that product of hate and misery. I had determined in my mind that the moment I was healthy enough, I would go back to Leszno. I was anxious about traveling in Poland since antisemitism had surprisingly come to the surface there. In fact, we heard about a recent pogrom in Kielce, where several Jews were killed and injured. Their possessions had been stolen or destroyed. How could this be? Did winning the war achieve nothing? I thought to myself, *What kind of insanity can make people act so stupid? Had they not learned a lesson from the hatred of the Germans, who had included them as victims?* I was driven. I needed to see if I could locate Lena and rescue her from that atmosphere of hate.

I went to the camp authorities, who were kind enough to help me get the necessary papers I needed to travel, as well as some money. I set out with hope in my heart but well aware that it would be a difficult trip of about 900 kilometers. The train ride was long, especially since I was so anxious to get to my destination and find Lena.

When I finally reached Leszno, I got off the train with my few possessions in hand and made my way to the street where I had grown up, delighted to be among such familiar sights. I stood and stared a long time at the house where my family and I had lived, unable to move, afraid of finding disappointment. Would anyone be there to recognize me? I was now 20 years old and fairly tall, not the gangly teenager they might remember. I knocked on the door and waited. No answer. I knocked a second time and then a third time, and finally I heard the door handle turn from the inside. I took a step back as a man opened the door just a crack, looked me over, and opened it wider. I could see his wife behind him. He studied me for a minute. "What do you want?"

"I am looking for my sister," I replied. "My family and I lived in this house. The Germans separated us. I don't want to bother you, but if I could come in for just a moment, it might help me remember things about where to find my sister."

"No," he said in a loud, firm voice. "This is our house now. Please leave." Then he asked, "Did you hide something here? Some valuables?"

"No, I am only looking for my sister."

"Goodbye then," he said and closed the door in my face.

I stood there for a moment, stunned and disappointed. With my thoughts in a whirl, I went to a small café and ordered a coffee. As I sat and sipped, I felt empty. Leszno was no longer the town I grew up in. I realized that there were no Jews here anymore. The bustle and activity they used to create was non-existent. Growing up here, days had been full of greetings and exchanging niceties with friends, families, and merchants. That warmth had disappeared.

As I sat in the coffee shop pondering my next step, I decided that I needed to figure out a starting place to search for Lena. I dimly remembered that Poppa had asked a Polish merchant who was a friend and who he trusted to take her in. He had paid the man to take that risk. But I just couldn't remember his name. Who could he be? I remembered there were two gentile Poles with whom he regularly did business. One was Mr. Lubinski, who owned a clothing store. The other was Mr. Kwalski, owner of a small department store. The clothing store was the closest, so I went there first. I found a woman sorting through clothes and asked for Mr. Lubinski. She told me to wait a minute and disappeared through a door in the back of the store. A middle-aged man who I'd never seen before came out.

"Who are you?" I asked. "I don't recognize you."

"We're even," he smiled. "I don't recognize you, either." He told me he was the owner of the clothing store and had purchased it two years ago from Mr. Lubinski. I apologized for being a bit blunt and introduced myself and told him why I was in Leszno. He said he was sorry but couldn't help me. My heart sank. I had only one option left. I thanked the owner of the store, and walked to Kwalski's department store, which wasn't far away.

As I entered his store, I recognized Mr. Kwalski immediately, but the look on his face said that he had no idea who I was. I think the smile on my face and the way I locked eyes with him pushed him to look more closely, wondering why this young man stood there staring at him. He had not seen me for about five years, but a warm smile of recognition blossomed as he finally recognized me. "Avrum Bielinski! Oh, my goodness! How are you?" He turned to his clerk and said, "We are going to the office. Please watch the store."

I followed Mr. Kwalski to his office, my mind dancing with a million thoughts.

"It is good to see you, Avrum. Would you like some tea?"

"Yes, thank you," I said and sat in the chair he offered me.

"Do you know anything about your parents? Are they still alive?"

I told him that I had learned from my friend, Symon, that my parents were gone.

His eyes became misty and he hung his head in sadness as he

clucked his tongue. "We were good friends, your father and I." He sighed. "I never had to worry when I did business with him. What can I do for you?"

"I am looking for my sister, Lena. The last thing I remember is that she was with you."

There was a moment of hesitation and then he told me the whole story. He explained how terrified his wife had been and how worried he was that a neighbor might report Lena to the German police. "I took her to a convent after talking with the Mother Superior, who reassured me that they would do all they could to keep her safe." He looked at me as if he wanted me to say something but couldn't.

I realized his dilemma. "You have a good heart, Mr. Kwalski. You did a good thing. I know my father trusted you and, under the circumstances, I would have done the same."

We paused in thought. An expression came to my mind: *If you're afraid of the answer, don't ask the question.* I was afraid of what I might hear, but I summoned my courage and asked him anyway.

"Is she there now?"

"No, but the sisters can tell you more than I can."

"I will go to the convent and see what I can find out about Lena."

I got up. Mr. Kwalski and I hugged. I thanked him and left, feeling I was on the right path. It was a long walk to the convent, and I looked forward to finding out more about my little sister.

A convent is an intimidating place if you have never been to one. This one was no exception. Built with heavy blocks of stone, it stood stoically, like a fortress. The massive, arched front doors, with oversized iron hinges, handles, and key locks, were open, so I just walked in. Inside, it was eerily quiet. The silence, surrounding me like a fog, made me feel alone and isolated. Sisters in the garb of their order quietly walked about, as if on a mission, giving no more than a quick glance at anything around them. It felt sterile to me, unlike the warmth of a Jewish Synagogue that I was used to.

As I thought about my next move, a voice behind me said, "May I help you?"

I turned to see a nun, clothed in her white habit.

"Yes," I replied. "May I please see Mother Superior?"

The nun asked me to wait for a moment and disappeared. A minute later, she came back with an older woman who was dressed similarly to the nun, except that she had a long, black vestment over her white outfit. "This is Mother Superior."

"What can I do for you?" Mother Superior asked.

"I am Avrum Bielinski. Mr. Kwalski in Leszno told me to see you. He brought you my sister, Lena, about five years ago. She was 12 years old at the time. I am looking for her. I have lost the rest of my family and she is all I have. Is she here?"

Her eyes became distant for a moment as her mind revisited that time in 1940. Then, she looked at me and shook her head. "No, I'm sorry."

"Can you give me any information about where I might find her?"

She thought for a minute and then unfolded the story of Lena's stay at the convent. At the end, she told me that Lena and her other Jewish friends had left to join a group of partisans hidden in the forest. She said that one of the girls had two brothers in the partisan group. Although it had been a hard decision, she had let them go.

"Do you know what group or what forest?" I asked.

"No," she answered. "I've told you everything I know. I'm sorry."

"Well, I cannot thank you enough for looking after her for the time she spent here. Bless you all. I need to keep searching."

We smiled and nodded at one another.

On my trip back to the DP camp, I marveled at the successful day: finding Mr. Kwalski at his store and then talking with the convent nuns who risked their lives for my little sister. I said a prayer for them all.

Returning from Leszno

I made my way back to the train station, having decided that I would try to find the nearest American-run DP camp, where friendly services and good information could be found. I hoped their lists would be more complete than those at Dachau. My trip to Leszno had been disappointing in one aspect, but at least it had provided me with some information about Lena. My body was still not completely recovered, and my mind was tired and confused. I would be able to relax on the train.

I couldn't get on the first train, which was too crowded, but I did get a seat on the second one. The journey would take a while, but I didn't mind. I needed time to think. As the train moved through Poland, I felt sick seeing the destruction of the war, especially in the small cities. Even the countryside was littered with remnants of the war.

I thought about how to find Lena. *Where could I go? Who could I ask?* At some point, I must also think of my own life. I had a duty to raise a family, to pass on the legacy of Jewish life. I needed a plan, one that I could successfully make happen. One I could control.

I decided to ask for advice at a different DP camp where there were agencies with trained people who could help me. I knew that the United Nations Relief and Rehabilitation Administration (UNRRA) would be a big help, as well as the Jewish Agency. I had heard of a camp called Feldafing, where everything I needed was available. I hoped I could get answers from the people around me about how to find Feldafing, but every face on the train looked hostile to me. I had to put aside my fears and start asking complete strangers for information. I thought I'd start with those people whose job involved answering questions. Perhaps the conductor, or, better yet, maybe the agent who took tickets could tell me how to reach my destination. To my relief, the agent couldn't have been nicer. He courteously and patiently gave me the information I needed.

I finally reached Feldafing, an all-Jewish camp. It was buzzing with activity. Originally, the DP camps serviced a mix of all types of people who had been displaced by the war, which meant that Jews and Jew-haters lived together. Many problems arose from the tension created by this situation, which eventually reached the attention of Harry Truman, President of the United States. He was furious at the mishandling taking place. Truman sent Earl G. Harrison, the Dean of the Law School at the University of Pennsylvania, to Europe to investigate these camps. Harrison, too, was appalled and shocked by what he found. He recommended that a large number of Jews be allowed to go to Palestine, a land controlled by the British at that time. This never happened in the numbers suggested by Harrison, but some Jews were allowed to go there, Jews who otherwise never would have had the opportunity. Based on Harrison's assessment, President Truman called for significant changes to the treatment of Jews in DP camps. These changes were implemented by General Dwight D. Eisenhower, who, by moving non-Jews to other camps, created mostly-Jewish and all-Jewish camps that were more peaceful, nurturing places.

Feldafing was full of action, providing all types of entertainment and distraction daily. One could choose between sports, music, or plays; the children enjoyed going to school; newspapers informed and educated us; different political groups, such as the Zionists and communists, were active and accessible, allowing freedom of choice and expression. The people looked healthy and happy. Weddings took place daily, a joyous sign for a battered people seeking normal, fulfilling lives.

After getting to know the camp, I found myself a place to sleep. I looked forward to a period of time of enjoying regular food and rest. The next day, I started checking out the various agencies, looking for family names and advice on where I could eventually live. While standing outside the United Nations Relief and Rehabilitation Administration office, I heard a man shouting my name. I looked to see where the voice was coming from. Suddenly, it was next to me.

"Avrum," gasped a young man, totally out of breath.

I was shocked. *Oh my God, it was my cousin Herschel, my Uncle Nathan's oldest son!*

We rushed into each other's arms and hugged intensely, both crying. "Herschel, oh Herschel, you are alive! Come, let us go where we can talk."

Herschel gave me news that confirmed what I knew about my parents and had suspected about the other members of our family. He had seen their names on a list of those murdered. They were gone. I didn't feel completely shattered, because Symon had already told me about my parents, and Herschel hadn't seen Lena's name on any list. I told him about my visit to Leszno.

"Avrum," he said, "I don't know what to tell you to do, but I think you must take care of yourself. My God, life is so precious, and now we have the ability, the opportunity, to create some sort of life for ourselves. You must do that. Poor Lena. We can't know what she went through, but you know, she may be all right. She might be creating her own life right now. Now that I have said that, I think, of course, you should continue your search for her."

We met several times. Then Herschel decided he would take his chances and go to Palestine. The Jewish Brigade had been helping people in any way they could, which impressed and motivated him. When the day came for us to go our separate ways, we hugged and said our farewells. We promised that we would try to find each other when we were settled. We reluctantly waved goodbye to one another as he walked away, suitcase in hand, headed to his new life.

Recuperating

Seeing Herschel was a good tonic for me. I generally felt better, but ghosts still haunted my mind. I decided to take a walk through Feldafing, as I often did, always hoping to see a familiar face. It was a really beautiful day. I saw a group of older men sitting around a table and decided to listen to what they were talking about. I edged up to the table and stood on the fringe, making it easy to hear the conversation.

One of the older men asked the others in the group, "So where does a Jew go from here?"

Another man replied, "How could anybody know? Even now we still have to look at barbed wire."

The first man answered. "Don't look down on our situation. We have people and agencies who are trying to help us. You know, I heard we are called *She'erit Hapletah*, the surviving remnant."

This comment was followed by a thoughtful moment of silence. Then, one of the men noticed me. "Young man, are you going to Palestine?"

I was unprepared to answer, but blurted out that I was not going there. Everybody in the group stared at me as if I should say something more.

Then one of the men asked, "Why, not? I understand you can receive help getting there, and where else would a young Jew go?"

"Father," I said to him, "there are many places that are possibilities, like America, or Canada, or Australia, or even South Africa, but those places are not too easy to get into because of quotas and restrictions. I'm sorry to say that the British are not too happy about Jews coming to Palestine."

"Too true," the man agreed.

"What I might do is try to go where I can find a relative, some family, if I am lucky enough to find that kind of situation. For now, I am looking for my little sister. That is a priority for me. What I can tell you is that I do not want to go back to Poland."

"Young man," said another gentleman, "they say there is a place called Kibbutz Buchenwald, right in the middle of Germany, where you can work on a farm with other young Jews. Sixteen young Jewish survivors of the war started this camp to prepare others for Zionism and a possible life in Palestine. Would you go to such a place?"

"I don't know anything about it, but it does not sound like a place for me. Frankly, I can't imagine being near anything German, let alone live in Germany."

The conversation continued, but thankfully, without me. Their questions and suggestions helped me refine my ideas on how Lena and I would continue our lives.

9

MOLLIE
MAY 1945 TO JULY 1945

An Adventure

One afternoon, Poppa Jan told me that Easter was coming, and we had to go to church. He said it was time to confess our sins. I had no idea what he was talking about. When I explained that I didn't know what he meant, he told me that Momma Zofia would explain it to me and help me. She was happy to educate me on Christian rituals and explained the whole confession process to me. I looked on blankly, trying hard to understand something so foreign to my own religious beliefs. She realized my dilemma and decided to abandon the lesson. Instead, she simply prepared me for going to church.

"You have to be careful," she said. "No one can know that you're Jewish. When you go into the confessional, you must pretend that you are unable to speak or understand Polish. That way, they can't ask you questions that could give you away. The priest is Polish and speaks some German, but I do not think he can understand Russian or Ukrainian. He will ask you in Polish to confess. Can you speak any Russian or Ukrainian?"

"I can speak Ukrainian fairly well because there were a lot of Ukrainian people in my hometown," I said.

"Then speak only Ukrainian. No Polish. He'll say something to you in Polish and when you answer him in Ukrainian, he may do what he can to communicate with you in Polish, even German. Then you pick the right time to say anything you want in Ukrainian. He'll probably think you're confessing and let you finish and leave."

Although I didn't really understand the idea of confession, I told her I could do this. She was clearly relieved that I understood enough to keep us all out of trouble.

Sunday arrived and we all dressed up and made our way to the church, a modest building with spires that reached to heaven. The beehive of people that had congregated there went inside and took seats in the pews. I sat right next to the confession booth, so I could eavesdrop on whatever others were confessing. Most of it was too soft to hear, but I could catch enough conversation to get an idea of what a confession should sound like.

When it was my turn to enter the confessional, I made up some sins and told them to the priest in Ukrainian, knowing he'd have no idea what I was saying. He asked me about my sins in Polish. I answered in Ukrainian that I didn't understand him. He plowed forward, urging me to confess my sins, and I rattled on with my made-up sins for a while. After some time, the priest interrupted me, saying something about Hail Marys and things I needed to say to atone for my sins.

"What a nice little room this is," I said in Ukrainian. "Do you come here often?"

He said goodbye to me in Polish and I left, happy that it was over, yet having had fun pretending that I couldn't speak Polish. It was scary but amusing at the same time.

While we were at the church, I heard some of the people whispering that the Russians were advancing toward our area and the Germans were falling back. No one wanted to say too much because there was the possibility of German sympathizers among us. I had given no thought to the war ever ending. In fact, I could not imagine what that could mean. I thought about Lena, the Jewish partisan girl I had met. I remember the feeling of comfort I had while being with her. When would I meet another Jewish person again?

The Warning

I had been working on Poppa Jan's farm for what must have been almost four years. I had lost track of time but always thought about my parents and my brother Yankel. I worried, wondering if they were alive, because of all the things I had heard about what the Germans had done to Jews. When we had gone to the market to sell our produce, I'd heard people talking and saying things that were hard to believe. No matter what I heard, I kept my mouth shut and listened. I only spoke when someone wanted some vegetables and Poppa Jan was too busy with another customer.

I had grown and matured and now noticed the young boys at the market looking at me with interest. I kept my head down and didn't look back, not wanting to encourage them, and just focused on our business.

Our last two visits to the marketplace had been a little different. I was aware of people whispering about Germany losing the war. Poppa Jan told me that there were Nazi sympathizers among the townspeople, so the less we said the better. There always seemed to be a few German soldiers at the market who bought some fruit and just wandered around. I could feel them take long looks at me occasionally. I made sure never to return the looks and to always seem busy.

One day, as we prepared to go to market, Poppa Jan's good friend, Piotr, came riding down the road on his horse, waving and shouting. "Jan, the Germans are leaving! They have orders! I am told they're going back to Germany. They are pulling out. The war isn't over, but the Russians are coming, I heard!" He leaned down and told Poppa Jan, "Hide your women. The Russians may save us from the Germans, but I heard they are barbarians and act like animals with the people they liberate. They steal and go after the women. Be careful!" Then he turned and rode away.

Poppa Jan called us all into the house and told everyone what Piotr had said. "The women must hide when the Russians come until they pass us by and move on. In the barn, there is a cellar, as you all know. Zofia, Catherine, and Mollie will go in there. Jerzy and I will pile straw over the trap door that covers it.

We all nodded that we understood.

"The Russians can have whatever food and drink they want," Jan continued, "but there may be no problem at all. I think their officers will try to keep their men under control, but we will be as cautious as we can."

Catherine and I looked at each other but said nothing. I thought: *From Poppa Jan's mouth to God's ear. Hopefully there won't be a problem.* How strange it was to now have to worry about our liberators.

The Russians Arrive

In the following weeks, we heard Allied bombers flying overhead on a regular basis. They usually flew over during the night, headed for God knows where. There was still a German presence throughout the countryside, though it was much lighter than it had been. At this time, the Poles and the Germans were getting along just fine, probably connected by their mutual hatred for Jews. Then, one day, the Germans seemed to vanish. Had they really left. Would they be back? We waited for the other shoe to drop.

I was in the field hoeing when I heard some vehicles coming. Seeing their insignias were clearly Russian, I grabbed my hoe and ran towards the barn. It was a long run, and I could see the Russian vehicles turn towards our house. I prayed that I could make it to the cellar in time, get in with Momma and Catherine and find safety there. As I ran into the barn, out of breath, I saw Jerzy covering up the opening to the cellar with hay and putting a horse yoke over the opening to disguise it. He looked at me, shocked.

"Where have you been? I thought you were in the cellar with Catherine and Momma."

Just then, a Russian armored car pulled up to the entrance of the barn, with a group of Russian soldiers following a short distance behind.

Jerzy grabbed me and whispered, "Stay quiet no matter what." He pushed me down into the bed of straw and quickly covered me with more straw and a few farm tools. Then, he sat down on me. I could hardly breathe. No sooner had he sat down than the door of the armored truck opened and a Russian officer climbed out. By now, the other foot soldiers caught up and came into the barn. When the officer saw Jerzy, he asked him a question in Russian. Jerzy smiled and shrugged his shoulders, as though he couldn't understand him, then fished a bottle of vodka from his coat and lifted it up high.

"Welcome, comrades!" he shouted in Polish.

The Russians looked at him, then to one another, their expressions agreeing that this was a drunken farmer.

"Come, join me!"

From his coat, Jerzy pulled out another bottle of vodka. He was prepared for just this sort of an encounter. The Russians, smiling at his foolishness and the temptation of the vodka, looked carefully around the barn as they stood around this drunken Polish fool. The officer spoke a little Polish. "Who are you?"

Jerzy gave him a look as if he couldn't understand the terrible accent of the officer and threw him one of the vodka bottles. He caught the bottle, saving it from falling to the ground and breaking.

"Who are you?" he asked again.

Jerzy looked back at him with a big smile and said, "I work for the farmer."

"Where are the women?"

"The women who work here only come a few days a week. They must be in the village now. Join me for a drink, comrade. Are the Germans gone?"

"Yes, we are sending them all back to Germany."

The officer turned to the soldiers and translated the conversation. Then he opened the vodka bottle, took a gulp and passed it around.

Hidden beneath Jerzy's heavy bottom, I was crushed, sweating, and all cramped up, but I never moved. The Russians took turns drinking from the bottle Jerzy had given them. Then, Jerzy pretended he had too much to drink and held his head, as though it hurt.

"Which way is the village and how far is it?" the officer asked.

"Uhm," Jerzy mumbled, "keep on the road. It's about ten kilometers. And please don't tell my boss I'm in here drinking."

The officer looked around one more time, then said something to his men, who immediately grabbed their weapons and turned to leave. He stopped for a moment and, holding up the empty vodka bottle, thanked Jerzy loudly in both Polish and Russian. He climbed back into the armored car, slammed the door shut, and rattled slowly down the road with his comrades following him. Under the straw, I heard the squeaking sound of the armored car's chain track grow softer and softer until there was silence. I flinched and Jerzy whispered to stay still. I did.

After about ten minutes, he got up and walked to the door just as Poppa Jan rushed in.

"Is everything alright?" Poppa Jan asked.

"Fine," said Jerzy. He poked me and said, "You can get up now, Mollie. They are gone."

We stayed on the farm for a week and saw no more Russian soldiers. A large group had terrorized the village with their drinking and plundering and worst of all, raping of any woman they could find, then they left. Meanwhile, the bulk of the Russian forces marched through Lodz in huge numbers on their way to Germany. They were an enormous army, but in many places they acted barbaric and out of control as they made their way through Poland.

God love Jerzy. The old man saved me from a horrible fate. I will always be grateful.

Having to Leave

The war had moved past our section of Poland. The Russians, after staying in our area for a few terrible days, pressed on to Germany and Berlin. Now it was just a matter of time and this brutal period would be over. I had come to the farm as an innocent girl and was now a mature young woman. I knew in my heart that as grateful as I was to Poppa Jan and Momma Zofia, I needed to move on and search my family, as many of them as I could find. I needed to resume my Jewishness and celebrate the Jewish holidays as my parents had taught me. It was odd to think this. For so many years I'd been frightened to even consider the idea of being openly Jewish. But it was time for me to figure out how I would be able to leave and where I would go. I knew I didn't want to travel alone, so I decided to ask Poppa Jan for his advice.

I waited until our regular trip to the marketplace to tell him that it was time for me to leave. He surprised me when he said he knew this day was coming, and though he knew I'd need to find my own way, he had hoped that I might decide to stay with him and Zofia. They'd grown to love me as their own. We both became teary-eyed talking about this. Neither of us could think of a plan that would get me to a destination that wasn't yet defined. We decided to talk about it at home, after the market was over.

All morning, I could barely do my work, my mind spinning over a plan to leave, and the frustration of not being able to come up with a destination. Then, in the early afternoon, three young men came to our stall to buy some fruit and vegetables. They were obviously not Polish, so Poppa Jan asked them where they were from. They said they came from Palestine and were here to recruit Jews to come to that land and settle down. They belonged to *Hashomer* Hatzair [the Young Guard]. Poppa Jan asked them where they would go next.

One of the young men, Zvi, answered him. "We are on our way to a displaced persons camp. We will find many Jews there and tell our story."

Poppa looked at me, winked, and asked the young men whether they would like to come to the farm for a hot dinner. The other two men, who had been stealing appreciative glances at me, nodded at Zvi enthusiastically and told Poppa that they would be delighted to share a hot dinner with such a nice family. I had learned to ignore admiring eyes, but this time I found myself feeling a bit flushed.

After the market, we all managed to squeeze into the horse-drawn wagon and rode back to the farm. Poppa introduced me to the young men, telling them my name was Mollie. The two admiring Palestinians, Ari and Eli, were attractive—each in a different way—and fun to be around. On the ride home we chatted and laughed as young people do. I absolutely loved it. Poppa Jan was strangely silent. Back home, we sat down to one of Momma Zofia's terrific dinners, the flavors of the food and conversation mixing like a perfect recipe for pleasure. The young men were openly grateful, while I was silently appreciative.

I wasn't aware of this, but just before dinner, Poppa Jan had secretly told Momma that the time had come for me to leave.

As dinner ended, Poppa Jan addressed the young men. "My friends, this dinner has been very special, and you young men have made it even more special. Because of that, I want to share a dilemma with you." The three Palestinians became quickly attentive, as Poppa Jan continued. "Our daughter, who we have adopted, has a destiny she must pursue. Mollie must go on journey as soon as possible to fulfill that destiny. I am asking you young men if you will take her with you and protect her until you reach the DP camp you spoke of. She is Jewish, and needs to know the fate of her true family."

Catherine and Jerzy gasped. I was surprised by his announcement. I had no idea he would take it this far. Somehow, he had made a decision for me that was perfect, one I couldn't make on my own. Zvi, who was obviously the leader, looked to his two friends for approval. They almost fell over themselves agreeing that it was a good idea and said they would happily take me with them. He smiled at his friends like a proud big brother, understanding how much they appreciated me and the opportunity to travel together.

The next morning, we arose early. I put my belongings in a cloth sack that I could easily carry, and Momma Zofia packed us food to take on our trip. Catherine and Jerzy were as teary-eyed as I was. Big Catherine gave me an unforgettable bear hug. Then Jerzy, with a sad, loving look, hugged me as well and gave me an affectionate kiss on the cheek. I thanked Momma and Poppa with hugs and kisses, our eyes filled with tears. They were as crushed as I was. They had saved my life. I told them I loved them, that I would not forget them and would do everything I could to contact them once I was settled. Poppa Jan, with a tearful smile, handed me a small purse containing some money. He said it was for the trip, to help provide security for me on my "unknown journey." I gave him and mama one last hug and kiss. Then the young men and I went on our way.

Traveling with the Palestinians

Our goal was to reach a displaced persons camp where the young men could recruit Jews for Palestine and where I could try to locate relatives. We hoped to make our way to an American DP camp somewhere in Germany, where the resources were better than in the Russian DP camps. The young men also realized that the Russians were pushing their communist doctrine and that didn't help them with recruiting Jews for Palestine. Palestine was run and controlled by the British, who were not happy to allow any more Jews into the country—even if they were survivors of German camps and brutality—because this could create a dangerous population shift.

Zvi asked me if I had my papers with me. *What papers?* It never occurred to me or to Poppa Jan that I would need papers. I told him I had none.

"Don't worry, Mollie, I have some here with me, meant for smuggling Jews into Palestine, when necessary. We'll fix them up for you."

The thought of forged papers made me nervous, but I was in the hands of supposed experts and needed to relax. Besides, the first stage of our journey gave me enough to think about. We walked a great deal, sometimes got rides with farmers, and rode in buses where possible. The buses were in terrible shape, with broken out windows and smoking engines. But they moved in the right direction, so they would do. It tore at my heart to see the Polish countryside—normally flowing and beautiful—in shambles wherever the Russians had driven their tanks and vehicles and marched their infantry on the way to the next destination.

I asked Eli what Palestine was like.

"It is very hot and sparse. There is a lot of sand and desert in many places. The foods there are quite different, and the farmers grow things like dates and pomegranates, which you do not find here."

I asked him if he was born there.

"No, I was actually born here in Poland, but my parents moved to Palestine when I was young. Zvi was born in Russia. His parents also moved to Palestine when he was young. Ari was born in Palestine. He is a sabra."

"A sabra?" I exclaimed. "What does that mean?"

"A sabra is a type of cactus that is tough and prickly on the outside and sweet on the inside. That's what native-born Palestinian Jews call themselves. They feel a kinship with the plant."

I liked his explanation and hoped I could go there someday. Talking with the young men made the time go faster and helped reduce the anxiety I felt, of wanting to get to my destination and reach my goal. Each of my companions was charming in a different way, but all of them were carefree and loose in the same way. I loved their freedom of expression, being able to talk about any subject without having to be careful with their words and thoughts.

Along the way, as we passed through a small village, we heard a commotion. We saw a boy of about ten years old being threatened by a group of about a dozen older boys. The gang was throwing stones at the boy and shouting curses at him. Zvi stepped between them and, giving a menacing glare at the group, asked what was going on.

"He is a Jew! He steals and is a Christ killer," one of the bigger boys shouted.

"How do you know?" Zvi asked.

"Know what?"

"That he is a Christ killer? Were you there?"

"How could I be?"

"So you don't know. Get away from here. Now!" Zvi demanded and took a threatening step toward the group.

The boys immediately backed off, turned and left, without putting up any kind of a fight. That was good. Zvi turned to the quivering young boy and asked if he was okay and who he was. The boy looked at the four of us. "Thank you. They would have hurt me badly if you hadn't helped. My name is Henrik Pomeranz." Then he straightened up, and with a flash of fire in his eyes answered defiantly. "I am Jewish and these peasant boys and most of their parents do not like Jews. I don't know where my family is or if they were taken away by the Germans. When they disappeared, I hid for a while, until this old lady found me and saved me. She took me in and I lived with her.

I helped her get around and I did errands for her. She was good to me. Then she got sick and died. I was alone again." The boy stopped abruptly. His eyes narrowed with suspicion. "Who are you?"

Zvi leaned toward the boy and answered loudly for anyone to hear. "We are Jews too. We are going to a displaced person's camp where there will be many more Jews. Would you like to join us?"

Henrik's face lit up. "Yes, yes, I would!" he blurted with a wide grin.

Our growing little band continued on our trip. The time passed in a blur until, tired and worn out, we finally reached the displaced person's camp of Feldafing.

10

LENA
OCTOBER 1945 TO JUNE 1946

We Move On

The sun shone on a very different world the morning after we heard the news that the war was over. It was hard to believe. All those years of hiding and living in the woods, the raids against the Germans, living life on a day-to-day basis, losing family and friends, gaining new friends and comrades—all of that suddenly froze in time. Now, The Parczew Foxes were disbanding and going their separate ways, either individually or in groups. After tearful goodbyes, hugs, and kisses, the partisan fighters, including me, had to address ourselves to the most difficult mission of all: planning the rest of our lives. Where would we go? What would we do with the guns? How would we live? Could we find our family and friends?

Schmuel, Meir, and Sol huddled together.

Sol turned to Schmuel and asked, "Do you have any plans? I know you have been thinking about this moment."

"You're right. I have given this moment a lot of thought. As I told our friends last night, I have no intention of staying in Poland and continuing to be abused. I would like to go to North America, where I understand that opportunities exist for a man to make something of himself. I am not sure of what I have to do to enter the US or Canada, because of the quotas they have, but I think I can work that out."

Meir listened attentively, his gaze fixed on his brother.

Schmuel continued. "Meir and I have an uncle in Canada who's in the trucking business and I think he would sponsor both of us, providing of course that Meir wants to go to there." Schmuel looked at Meir with a questioning look on his face.

Meir did not hesitate. "Brother," he said, "you are all I have. You and I are luckier than many other families because we've had each other in these difficult times. I've thought about Palestine, but like you, I grew up and have lived in and around the forest for a long time. Sand and desert are not for me. Canada is appealing to me, if we can arrange to get in."

Schmuel looked at Meir with a brother's glowing love and nodded. "What about you, Sol?" he asked. "Do you have an answer?"

Sol smiled at his good friend. "Yes," he said. "I, too, have given it a lot of thought. I'm inclined to go to what they tell me is the Promised Land, Palestine, and see for myself what a little bit of milk and honey tastes like, if indeed it does exist. In fact, boys, I'm going to ask Anna to go with me."

Smiles broke out on the faces of both Schmuel and Meir. "Mazel tov, Sol!" they both congratulated him at once.

Sol held up a hand. "Schmuel, since I have told you about Anna and me, I have to ask you what will happen with you and Lena?"

"That's a great question and an easy answer. I intend to ask her to marry me. She fills my life with wonder."

Sol and Meir shot glances at one another with stunned smiles.

"Her only relative that might still be alive is her brother, Avrum. We'll look for him and maybe we can find him."

"Have you told her how you feel? Does she know how you feel?" Meir interrupted. "My brother knows about a lot of things, but with women he is no smarter than a turnip. I suspect she knows, but it's up to you to get that business taken care of."

Schmuel smiled broadly. "My friends, what I think we have determined here is that we need to get to where there is a British presence. Meir and I wish to go to Canada and you, Sol, are heading to Palestine. Since Canada is part of the Commonwealth, and Palestine is controlled by the British, who are the creators of the Commonwealth, it would make the most sense to deal with the British."

Meir and Sol listened attentively, agreeing with Schmuel's logic.

"I've heard of another concentration camp that has been converted to a displaced persons camp. It's run by the British. It's called Bergen-Belsen. But we'll have to travel through Poland and a part of Germany to reach it. I have no doubt how difficult that could be. I propose we think about it today, and sleep on it. Then, we'll make our plans in the morning when our minds are fresh and figure out the best way to get there."

Meir and Sol nodded and the three went off into the night to their sleeping places.

Making Plans

The forest air felt brisk and clear when the Jewish partisans awoke the next morning. On this second day after the war ended, the camp looked smaller, leaner, more obviously disassembled. The partisans, their possessions, and camp materials had dwindled significantly. After breakfast, those still in camp discussed their potential plans with their compatriots, who they had shared their lives with these last few years. Some had already left, some wanted to leave as soon as they could, and others were not in a hurry. All were concerned about what they would find out about the state of their families. Schmuel got together with Sol and Meir to discuss their forthcoming plans.

Meir spoke up first. "Don't you think we should have the girls here with us while we're making plans?"

Schmuel nodded. While the women were treated well by the men in camp, the men still made the major decisions, and the women supported those decisions without question. He cautioned his friends not to mention to Lena that he was going to ask her to marry him. He would ask her soon, he said, but not now. Meir volunteered to get Lena and Anna and took off immediately to find them. A few minutes later he returned with the girls in tow. When they were all together,

Schmuel explained to them that they were going to leave Poland and make their way to the British to seek help with their immigration to Canada and Palestine.

"Schmuel, what of my brother and our other relatives?" Lena immediately asked. "Perhaps they are in Poland, and we will leave them behind."

"We will do everything we can to locate our families. I'm sure the British have the resources to locate people much better than we can."

She nodded. All eyes were fixed on Schmuel. They all trusted him in the same way a child trusts a parent. They looked to him for guidance.

Schmuel continued. "I think it would be best for us to travel by bicycle as far as we can. Hopefully, we can hitch rides wherever possible and gather information along the way. Obviously, we'll have to scrounge for food and shelter, which is nothing new for us. We'll be five dirty, poorly clothed Jews traveling in a sometimes unfriendly climate. Does anyone have any suggestions or comments?"

They all looked at one another.

Sol spoke up. "I agree with everything you've said. I might add that we should carry a gun or two for protection, which I hope we won't have to use."

"Let's spend the day planning the trip," Schmuel suggested, "and make sure we bring everything we'll need. I think we can safely plan to leave tomorrow morning,"

As they got up to leave, Schmuel put his hand on Lena's shoulder and asked her to stay for a minute. The rest of the group knew what was about to happen and turned away from the couple, taking long steps to leave and give them their privacy. Schmuel coughed and cleared his throat. "I've been wanting to talk to you, Lena."

"About what?"

"Well, you've grown into a beautiful young woman. When I'm with you, I'm relaxed and comfortable. That's a delightful thing."

"Yes, it is," Lena agreed, wondering where Schmuel was going with this.

"When we start this journey, it will be for the rest of our lives."

Schmuel paused, his mouth and throat dry with tension. "Lena, I love you and I want you to be in my life forever."

Her eyes widened and tears welled up. *Could this be what I think it is?*

"Will you marry me, so we can share the rest of our lives together?" The briefest moment of silence took place, each savoring the words. "If this idea pleases you, we will find a rabbi somehow somewhere and our friends and God will be our witnesses—"

Lena reached out and took Schmuel's rough hands in hers, pulling them to her thumping heart. "Yes, Schmuel, I will marry you gladly," she said softly. "I trust you and respect you, and I have loved you for a long time."

They both smiled broadly. Their emotions spilled out as they hugged one another tightly and enjoyed a long, sweet kiss. This had been an especially good day in the forest.

Before the Journey

The night before they were supposed to start their journey, the young Jewish partisans sat in their respective beds, reflecting on what had happened in each of their lives in these past few, war-ravaged years. Anna, who had fought in the ghetto and had been captured and interned at the Sobibor death camp only to escape and join the partisans, was already an old soul, even though she was only 19 years old. She had no idea if any of her brothers, sisters, or parents were still alive. She was angry at the Nazis for all the death and pain she had witnessed. In the time spent with the partisans, she had gained stability and purpose. And she had found Sol. Sol gave her hope and the comforting assurance that someone cared. Together, they would try to go to Palestine and be part of what would hopefully be a Jewish homeland. Though she loved the forest and its protection, peace, and serenity, she knew the time had come to move on. She thought about her own hopes and dreams, looking deep within herself to find what she really wanted and needed. She realized that she wanted a family of her own, to raise children in a world without Nazis, prejudice, or hate. She sighed and said to herself, *Anna, it's time to move ahead to* a new and better life. I hope I won't not lose contact with my dear friend, Lena. Then, she drifted off to sleep.

Sol looked forward to the next morning when the journey toward the rest of his life would begin. In the war, he had teamed with Schmuel to put together a small band of Jewish partisans and was proud of that. In his previous life, he had been a schoolteacher and the leadership skills he developed in that profession had quickly been realized by the partisans. It would be hard to leave Schmuel and Meir, who he had known most of his life, but now he had Anna. Together they would be part of building a Jewish homeland. He had never been able to understand what the Jews had done to generate so much hatred towards them. Sol decided that the last generation, right or wrong, teaches the next generation what they know, even if what they pass along is without fact or substance. He decided he would do his best to avoid being caught up in the sickness of hate. With a partner like Anna, he could do great things. Tomorrow would be a special day.

All his life, Meir had been a younger brother. He was dedicated to Schmuel, but also felt the need to create a life for himself. He was very proud to have been part of the Jewish partisans led by his brother and Sol. They had fought the German war machine and survived. Now, it was time to consider what he should do with the rest of his life. He thought that if he would go to Canada or another friendly country, he would want to have a family and teach them how to be Jews without fear. *I hope Schmuel and I can be partners in some business venture,* he mused. *I think I need to find a wife,* he chuckled to himself, *or maybe she'll find me! I'm ready to move on. I can't wait for tomorrow.*

What a day tomorrow will be, Schmuel thought. *It'll be the start of the rest of our lives. Even though I have been a child of the forest, I need to have an open mind now and look into the future. How lucky I am to be able to start a new life with Lena. I'm so glad we're leaving Poland. It's sad that these people don't want us here. They don't even seem to care that we fought the Nazis and many of us died for this country. There have been some Poles who have been good to us and I will always be extremely grateful to them. Yes, I have a lot to remember. I'm so excited to finally get going. Sol and Anna will go to Palestine, and I respect that. It's a temptation for me, too, but I think my future is with Lena and Meir in a place other than Palestine. Lena and I will raise a family in a Jewish community. I hope we will do well enough to help other Jews who need help, wherever they may be.* That was a beautiful thought on which to end his day.

As Lena tried to sleep in the Parczew forest for the last time, her excitement about the next day overwhelmed her. She was happy to leave the forest—especially the lice and sickness that bred here. She'd miss her comrades and friends and all that they had shared together. She'd miss the trees and lakes and the protection the forest gave them, but she knew that Schmuel would take them to a better place, a better life. She was happy to leave Poland, but sad to say that she never got to know this land. The Nazis took away the best of her teenage years and now she was almost 18 years old. She knew she wanted to raise a Jewish family and cook Shabbos dinners. She wanted to raise children and grow old playing with her grandchildren. She didn't know what had become of Momma and Poppa and had no idea where Avrum could be or if he was even alive. She promised herself to look for all of them when she could. On that note, she gave into her need for sleep and become one with the silent forest.

The Journey

Day number three of postwar peace arrived: the day when this group of five partisans would leave the camp and the forest forever. They were more than ready to go. Enough of the planning already, it was time for action. They had their breakfast together and said their goodbyes to the remaining partisans. Each member of Schmuel's group packed their bicycle with a small bag of food and a cloth sack with a few extra clothes. Each of the three men carried a pistol, hidden out of sight, which they hoped they would not have to use. All of them had a small amount of money. Enough, they hoped, to see them through to their destination: Bergen-Belsen. They would need to get to the German border, which was controlled by the Americans and British along with some units of the German civil police. Anyone who wanted to enter Germany was required to have the proper papers. Schmuel knew this would be a problem but had ideas on how to handle it when the time came. He figured that the only way to get around the law was to break the law and sneak across the border any way they could.

They soon realized that they weren't in good enough physical shape to ride their bicycles for long periods of time. Breaths were short and undernourished, aching muscles used up their oxygen quickly. After a great number of cycling and rest periods, they stopped for a quick lunch. Afterwards, they continued cycling. They were lucky because the landscape was relatively flat with very few hills. Pedaling and coasting became a technique to move forward for longer periods of time.

Living in the forest had given them some advantages, but also posed disadvantages. While it provided them with plenty of territory and places to hide, it didn't give them access to food, weapons, or clothing. Every advantage seemed to be paired with a disadvantage.

While it was best to avoid contact with others, which could possibly give them away, cycling with other travelers around them, mostly going in the same direction, would allow them to blend into the crowd. The first evening, after a long day of cycling, they found a small, wooded area that reminded them of the Parczew forest. They decided to make a small camp there and spend the night.

The road had been filled with travelers who also seemed to be looking for a new home. They could see a few campfires around them, probably from other refugees settling in for the night. Schmuel, always cautious, decided with Sol that they should keep someone on guard. They each took a two-hour shift watching and guarding the campsite while the others slept.

The next morning they ate a quick breakfast and were on their way. They did more cycling than walking since everyone's muscles were sore, and it felt easier to pedal the bicycles than walk. Around noon, while driving through a small village, they saw a small café and decided to stop and have lunch there. It felt like a dream to have access to a broad menu and to be waited on. After they ordered and were served their food, they noticed the local people staring at them with suspicious eyes. It was uncomfortable.

"They think that we are Jews," Meir whispered.

Sol chuckled. "Meir, they're right! And who cares?"

This was the first time in five years they had been served food in a café. What a pleasure! They ate, paid their bill, and left as the local people rudely stared after them. They spent the rest of the day pedaling as if in a trance, hardly stopping to rest. They noticed that the traffic on the road steadily increased as they approached the German border. At the first sight of the border, Schmuel signaled the group to pull over at what looked like a good resting place because others were already standing together there. The new group looked like a family. Schmuel walked up to them and asked where they were going.

"We are going to a displaced persons camp, we hope," an older man of the family group replied. "But we need papers to cross the border and we don't have them."

"What will you do?" Schmuel asked.

"Right now, I'm not sure. These people with me are the remnants of my family. We are luckier than most to have any family still alive. We'll try and get papers from somewhere. If we can't, we'll find a way across the border when it gets dark. We've come too far to quit."

"Do you know what camp you want to reach?"

"No, but it will be better than living on the road."

Schmuel smiled and nodded. "Go with God and good luck to you." He returned to his little partisan group, who anxiously asked him what happened. He told them of his conversation and said he had come to a conclusion. "It looks like we might have to leave our bikes and cross the border through the forest at night, in the darkness. The forest is too dense and overgrown for simple bike riding.

"We are forest people, and we can do it. I'm sure," Meir offered.

"I'll give it some thought. If we do need to leave the bikes, the rest of the journey might not be so bad. After we've crossed, we can walk to our destination, unless we get lucky and maybe catch a ride or two. Now, my little group of Jewish partisans, let's get some sleep."

The Service

Schmuel leaned against a fence post at the edge of a large, unplanted field where the group had parked their bicycles. He was preoccupied, thinking about the best way to cross the German border, when Meir walked up to him. "Schmuel, is there something wrong?"

"Not really," he responded. "I was just trying to sort out the best way to get to our destination in Germany from here. If we tried to do it legally, we'd have to apply for permits, but that would involve waiting for them to be okayed. Besides, three of us are carrying guns, which I really don't want to have to give up. I would feel better knowing that we could protect ourselves with these weapons. In the last village, where we had lunch, I heard people talking about a pogrom in a town called Liecse, where 46 Jews were murdered and many others injured. It makes me sick to hear that this type of hatred and stupidity still exists in Poland. It reinforces my desire to leave the country. We're not safe here. So I want to hang onto our guns, which the border police would surely take from us if we try to cross over legally."

From where he stood, Schmuel saw a good-sized stand of trees at the corner of an unplanted field just off the road and decided it would be a good place to camp for the night. The partisans moved to the grove of trees and were setting up camp when they saw the same old man that Schmuel had been talking to earlier approaching them with his family. The partisans stopped moving and waited for the family to reach them.

"Hello, again. Do you know what tonight is?" the old man asked.

The partisans looked at each other with blank expressions.

"It's Shabbos," the old man announced. "Sabbath is here. If we join together, we can have a service. I have four with me: two men and two women. You have five with you, including two women. That gives us only five men for a minyan. Of course, we need ten, but that's better than nothing." He paused. "I assume you're Jewish. You seem too smart to be anything else," he grinned.

The partisans stood quietly, no one wanted to comment. Then Meir stepped forward and in a voice louder than normal said,

"Mister, I think the idea for a Shabbos service would be wonderful. I had forgotten what day of the week it was. However, let me tell you something. As far as I am concerned, these women can be part of this. They fought with pride to be Jews, so they have earned the right to be part of a minyan. Your four and our five make nine and God makes ten. I would say we have a minyan!"

"Bless you, you are right!" The old man brightened.

The two groups gathered together and pooled their resources to create a more spiritual atmosphere. They had some candles, which the girls could light for Shabbos. The privilege to lead the service was given to Sol. There were no prayer books, so he closed his eyes, reached back into his war-weary memory and began singing. "*Sh'ma Yisrael, Adonai Elohanu, Adonai Echod.*"

He opened his eyes and looked upward. "Hear O Israel, the Lord, our God, the Lord is one. Cause us to lie down in peace, our God, and lift us up, restored to life."

Lena's eyes filled with tears as she remembered her family and the wonderful Shabbos services and dinners they used to have. Memories flooded to her during the entire service.

When it was over, everyone felt a great lift in spirit. They hugged one another and wished each other good luck and a good life. The family then moved on, waving goodbye as they left, and disappeared into the night. The partisans cleaned up, and bedded down, feeling soothed by their first Shabbos in years.

Crossing the Border

The morning sun had barely lit the campsite before the partisans were back on the road again. It was time to cross the border into Germany without papers. Serious business. When they moved closer to the border, they noticed how the traffic had thickened and filled the road. Schmuel was happy about that because this made them less noticeable. Now they would take the less traveled road that followed the border. At the small village right next to the border station, they stopped to buy sausages, cheese, and bread. Then they retired to a quiet spot on the side of the road to eat and make their plans.

"I think you are all aware that we will have to cross the border at night, away from the border police," Schmuel said. "We will have to get off this road and find a place that is more secluded."

They all nodded.

"In the last village, I bought a wire cutter in case we have to cut through a fence. If there is such a fence, then hopefully it is not connected to an alarm system. I think the border is too long to have every bit of it electrically wired. The nights have been cloudy, so that should diminish being lit up by the moonlight. It should be nice and dark. I'm told there are two more small villages ahead of us. At the next one, we'll need to sell our bikes. Once we've gotten through the forest and crossed the border, we can try and hitch a ride or we'll have to walk. Now, let's quietly leave the road and look for the best place to cross. Are there any questions or comments?"

Sol raised his hand. "I think it would be a good idea to look for a place in the middle of the two towns. I would think that most border patrols would take place closer to the villages."

"That's a good thought. That's what we'll do. We'll explore the area that's in between the two villages and go to the border there. Anyone else?"

No one spoke.

"Let's go then."

The five moved onto the road and made their way to the next village. It would be a long day.

When they saw the lights of the village, they stopped in a nearby field and set up camp. In the morning, they awoke, ate, and made their way to the village. There, Meir asked where he could find someone who sold or repaired bicycles. He was given two names and addresses. Half of the group went to one address, the rest to the other. Since they were willing to sell the bicycles for next to nothing, both partisan groups successfully sold the bikes. They met at the center plaza of the village. Schmuel had asked his bicycle dealer how far it was to the next town. He shared that information when he got back to the group.

"Only 20 kilometers?" Sol laughed. "This is like a walk in the park. Except that it's a forest." The group joined him in laughter.

Walking ten kilometers to the halfway point between towns couldn't have been easier for the partisans who easily covered that sort of distance often in the war. They decided to kill time in the village and then walk back to the halfway point between towns in the late afternoon where they would enter the forest. They would travel at night. The group sat around the main square, visited a coffee shop for a few hours, and looked over the outskirts of the village. When the time was right, they headed out on the road.

The night was crisp and, as Schmuel had hoped for, overcast. As the group got closer to the entry point, they quietly moved off the road and made their way to the border. Meir's suggestions had worked out perfectly so far. The road they traveled on had been quiet and void of traffic. The pathway to the border was also nicely isolated.

When they reached the border, they were delighted to see a wire fence. The partisans lay silently in the grass for over an hour to make sure that there was no other human traffic near them. Then they moved to the fence. Schmuel took out his wire cutters and clipped a few strands. He stopped and listened. Nothing moved. There was no noise. He continued cutting until there was an opening big enough for Sol, the largest member of the group, to crawl through. He motioned for Sol to lead the way. Suddenly, they heard a dog barking and froze. Then there was silence again. They moved forward, stopping periodically to listen and orient themselves. With acute awareness, not unlike the raids they did regularly during the war, they moved quietly as a team, almost noiseless. Years in the forest had made them skilled in their movements.

They picked their way through the forest for almost two hours. Then Schmuel broke the silence. "I think we are in a safe place now. We're quite far beyond the border, so let's find a spot to stay the night. We can continue our trip tomorrow. Bergen-Belsen is still a good distance away. If we find a main road, perhaps we can get a ride to take us closer."

Everyone was happy to stop and rest, and, more importantly, happy to be on the other side of the border and past the police.

To Bergen-Belsen

We woke up with a great sense of relief now that we were out of Poland and into Germany, closer to Bergen-Belsen. We ate a small breakfast of stale bread and raw potatoes and made our way to a main road. Sol suggested that it would be faster if we purchased some bicycles. The group agreed. In the next village, we bought four bikes, which were all the bikes available. The group continued on, each person on a bike and Anna riding double with Sol. Unfortunately, the bikes weren't in good condition, so the group had to stop periodically to repair them. Still, we carried on, determined to reach our goal in the shortest amount of time.

Whenever we were among people, on the road or in a village, the atmosphere of civilian attitudes in Germany felt dark and heavy. People walked slouched over with their heads down with vacant eyes that stared at nothing. Everywhere they looked they saw the destruction from the Allied bombings punctuated by the rusty skeletons of military vehicles that lay next to the roads like carcasses of dead animals. Children cavorted in the rubble, the only play area available. Sadness hung in the air. We kept on the move, pressing forward, getting closer to our destination every hour.

Finally, Sol's bike broke down beyond repair. Meir said that his own bike was pretty much finished, as well. They knew this was going to happen, so they were mentally prepared to start walking. We ditched the bikes and, after a brief rest, got on the main road to try to hitch a ride. This day, luck was with us. We saw an English two-and-a-half-ton lorry with military markings coming down the road. At closer range, we could read the signage: Jewish Brigade Group. Schmuel ran out into the middle of the road, waving his hands with excitement. The truck stopped and the driver rolled down the window, studying the smiling faces of the five raggedy people.

He asked in English, "What can I do for you?"

Sol, who knew a few English words, shouted, "We are Polish and we are Jews." He felt a chilling shudder run through his body at saying the words aloud that would have gotten him killed in previous circumstances.

The driver stopped the engine and got out of the truck with his assistant. The canvas in the back of the truck parted briskly and two more soldiers jumped to the ground with rifles slung over their shoulders—a peaceful sign. Each of the four soldiers had an insignia patch on his left shoulder with a yellow Star of David sewn onto it. The men looked curiously at the bedraggled travelers. One of them stepped forward and, in perfect Yiddish, asked where we were going.

Sol replied in Yiddish, "We are trying to reach Bergen-Belsen. We want to go to the displaced persons camp there. Two of us want to go to Palestine and three of us want to go to Canada, if that's possible. We need help with that."

The driver answered in Yiddish. "We can help you, especially the two who want to go to Palestine. We're going to Bergen-Belsen ourselves."

Sol beamed with delight.

"My name is Elijah, the driver said. "My assistant driver is Bernie, and the two riding in the back are Moshe and Uri. Climb into the back and we'll be on our way."

Our exhausted but happy group clambered into the back of the truck with Moshe and Uri. Starved for information, we fired questions at them all at once. We all chattered like a flock of Yiddish magpies as the truck bounced down the war-torn road, toward a once-dim dream that had suddenly gained in brightness.

Arriving at Bergen-Belsen

The Jewish Brigade soldiers had not met any Jewish partisans yet and were fascinated by the concept of Jews fighting back. Most of what they knew about the war centered on the ghetto fighters and the slaughter of Jews in the camps. The ride was bumpy and erratic. The roads were in terrible shape, but that didn't slow down the conversation. Meir asked if there was a rabbi at the DP camp. Uri replied that there was and added that the DPs had set up schools, as well as a form of government there to maintain law and order. He asked Meir why he had inquired about the rabbi and Meir told him that Sol and Anna, as well as Schmuel and Lena, wanted to get married.

Moshe laughed. "You know they have on average 20 weddings a day there. People who didn't even know each other a week before are getting married. In addition to the many marriages, babies are being conceived at an incredible rate. God bless the Jews. They love life."

The truck hit a pothole and the riders bumped off their seats into the air, heaving a big moan in unison. Then, the truck slowed down and came to a stop. Moshe and Uri grabbed their rifles and jumped off the end of the truck to see what was going on. They suddenly became aware of two young men in ragged clothes standing on the side of the road, staring at them.

Elijah swung his rifle into a ready position. "Who are you?"

The two stood silent for a moment and then saw the Jewish Brigade insignia. Tears filled their eyes. "Brother, we are Jews trying to make our way to a place where we can get food and care," the taller of the two answered. "Then it's our goal to continue on to a better place than this miserable land."

"Where have you been?" Elija asked.

"We have been in German satellite work camps. My friend here was working in a munitions factory and I worked in a place where the Germans were making V-2 rockets. The American and British bombers unloaded on us regularly. Both Germans and Jews were killed in their attacks. We escaped and found each other. We have been wandering ever since."

"What are your names?"

"I am Dov Liebowitz and my friend here is Zymon Yoran. I am Polish and Zymon is Hungarian."

"Well then, come join our traveling circus."

Elijah motioned to the vehicle, and everyone clambered into the back of the truck. We resumed our journey. The ragged boys couldn't help but stare at the girls for a moment.

"Where are we going?" Dov asked.

"To Bergen-Belsen," replied Uri.

"What's it like?"

Uri glanced at Moshe and nodded towards him that he should

answer the question. "It was originally a Nazi training camp," Moshe said. "Then it became a labor camp. At one time the Germans held Jews hostage with the idea of exchanging them for German prisoners of war. The camp was liberated in April 1945, by the British 11th Armored Unit. The British discovered approximately 60,000 prisoners who were in terrible shape and another 13,000 corpses—all Jews. There were big problems with typhus, but the camp has been cleaned up and the displaced persons—almost entirely made up of Jews—have turned it into a vibrant and valuable stop to recover their health before moving on to new lives."

The truck stopped. Elijah appeared at the tailgate. "Who would like to eat? We have a couple cases of rations."

Our group and two survivors felt as though a miracle had taken place. Anna and I jumped up to help hand out the food. We ate in silence, giving thanks with every bite.

With full stomachs and the enjoyment of new companions, we went along our way, savoring our much-improved mood. Time passed much more pleasantly and before we knew it, we were at the gates of Bergen-Belsen. Once we entered that gate, the others went their separate ways while we partisans stayed together.

Preparing for Our Next Life

Bergen-Belsen seemed like heaven to us. We cleaned ourselves with hot showers and soap, were given fresh clothing—some of it new—and ate a hot meal. The Jewish Brigade soldiers had shown us to the camp administration building, where we were assigned living quarters. When the camp was liberated in April 1945, the British had immediately burned down the old barracks as a health precaution, because of the typhus. Now, in new, clean barracks, the British divided the men and women into separate groups for lodging.

Schmuel found it odd that the camp continued to use the name of what was once one of the largest and most frightening concentration camps. He learned that when the British decided to rename the camp "Hohne" the survivors protested and insisted on keeping the original name. He assumed that they wanted the world to remember the horrors of the concentration camps and know that something this grotesque could be changed into something positive and nurturing through good will and courage.

Bergen-Belsen provided an opportunity to meet new people, whether one wanted to or not. The camp was so crowded that there was no such thing as privacy. The residents came from many nations, including Poland, Hungary, Latvia, Lithuania, Holland, and Czechoslovakia. None wanted to go back to their original countries and face either antisemitism or the communist Russians. Many were still sick and had not recovered from the brutality of the Germans.

Yet, they had somehow made their way to this camp, where they could be rehabilitated and given the pathway to a new life. With the help of military authorities and many Jewish organizations, these survivors had put together their own schools and government and even started newspapers and orchestras. The Red Cross helped them, along with the United Nations Relief and Rehabilitation Administration, as well as the Organization for Rehabilitation Through Training (ORT), and the Joint Jewish Distribution Committee. Though language classes were compulsory, the most commonly spoken language was Yiddish.

Schmuel and I, as well as Sol and Anna, were married by an English Army chaplain. Eight other young couples got married on the same day. I couldn't believe that I had finally reached this day. It was glorious. We settled into camp life and worked on making a plan to continue our journey towards a brighter future. Schmuel and Meir had located an uncle on their mother's side in Canada and sent off letters and telegrams with the UNRRA's help. Canada had decided to implement a bulk labor program and accept qualified laborers and close relatives of existing Canadian citizens.

Sol and Anna were in constant contact with their friends in the Jewish Brigade. Early one evening Elijah and Moshe came to them.

"My friends, say your goodbyes," Elijah said. "Late tonight we are taking a group out of here to help them on their way to a seaport in Italy. You are part of that group. There will be a ship waiting to take you all to Palestine. Whether it gets there, we cannot guarantee, but

God willing, you will feel the sand of our Promised Land beneath your feet. Take only what you need and be back here at 11 p.m."

Sol and Anna raced to find the rest of us fellow partisans. Breathless, they told us the news. Then, we hugged and kissed one another with tears flowing and hearts beating with joy.

"We must never forget each other," Schmuel said, "and we must never forget we are Jews. Go with God, and may we someday see each other again in good health and peace."

Then they parted. There was a terrible void without Sol and Anna, but life had to go on. Schmuel, Meir, and I volunteered for various jobs, worked hard, and enjoyed having our work appreciated. Our search for family and friends never faltered as we checked with the authorities to see if they could find the names of any of our family members who had possibly survived, but we had no luck.

One day, Schmuel was summoned by the administration office. He walked in and identified himself, whereupon the clerk at the desk handed him an envelope. He waited until he was outside the office, then opened the envelope and quickly scanned its contents. He immediately took off on a dead run to where I was working, holding the letter in the air. I saw him coming, looking excited and almost childlike with his hand-waving motions.

"What's the matter?"

"Let's find Meir and celebrate! We're going to Canada!"

11

MOLLIE
JULY 1946 TO DECEMBER 1946

Feldafing

When my three Palestinian escorts and I reached Feldafing, we were greeted at the gate by American soldiers who asked if we had papers. We said we did, quickly found our papers, and presented them to the soldiers. My heart was beating in my mouth, but there were other travelers at the gate, anxious to get in, so the soldiers rushed us through. The compound was impressively large and surrounded by barbed wire, which struck me as an uncomfortable vision. There were a lot of people milling around the yard in various stages of quiet thought and active chatting. Zvi walked up to a small group and asked where we had to go to register. An elderly man gave us directions and the four of us went to a building to sign in. I was assigned to a women's building, while Zvi, Eli, and Ari were assigned to the men's section. After receiving our assignments, we stepped outside.

Eli took me aside. "Mollie, tomorrow we will be moving on as fast as we can so we can get to our homes in Palestine. We will miss you. I hope you can find at least some of your family. Hopefully all of them. There is a building here where they have people who can help you look and give you information."

I choked up as each of the young men stepped forward and gave me a warm hug. Then they went off to their barracks and I went to mine to settle in. They would be gone in the morning, headed home to Palestine. I would continue trying to make my own future, wherever that might be.

After the long journey with the Palestinians, I was exhausted and spent some time just meeting people and relaxing. It was a treat to be surrounded by so many Jews, but now I wanted and needed to stay busy, to be productive. I went to the headquarters building and volunteered to help in any way I could. They assigned me to the hospital to help with patients who had lost their way mentally. There were plenty of those. I felt useful and welcome. Being busy helped me to deal with the passing time.

I had put off looking for family names, fearing that I would find no one had survived, but now I finally went to the building that housed personnel and services dedicated to locating people. A very nice lady asked if she could help and, of course, I thanked her and told her I was looking for lost family.

"What names are you looking for?" the lady asked.

"I am looking for the Abramowicz family."

She pulled out a big book and started looking through a frighteningly long list of names. "Ah," she said, "I have a few Abramowiczes here." She turned the book toward me, pushing it closer to me.

I shook my head, muttering "No" over and over again as I scanned each name, each page. Then I saw the name "Yankel". My eyes widened and I became lightheaded. "That's my brother! He's alive?"

"Oh, yes," she replied. "In fact, he is here at Feldafing."

"Oh my God!" I blurted, feeling a giant wave of warmth run through my body. "How can I find him?"

The lady gave me directions to where Yankel was billeted. "That's where he sleeps," she said.

I thanked her profusely and started walking. When I arrived at his barracks, I saw a group of men playing chess. None of them was Yankel. I asked if any of them knew him and, if so, where he could be found. They all looked up from the intense chess game. One of the men told me that they didn't know where he was, but thought he'd return for sure in a little while.

I was disappointed and decided I would wait a while. If he didn't return, I'd come back later. A thousand thoughts raced through my mind, from little pieces of our childhood together, things he said and did, friends and work camp rumors. I took a big breath, feeling overwhelmed. After a half an hour, Yankel had still not shown up. I decided to leave and return later. As I walked away, I heard my name being shouted. "Mollie! Mollie Abramowicz!"

I spun around to see Yankel running toward me, looking full of life and healthy, his face overjoyed. He raced up to me and grabbed me in a big hug. Choking on words, we held each other tightly, as though if we let go, the other might float away and disappear forever.

"Oh, Mollie, my dear sister, you are really here! It's just you and me, and we have survived. We have so much to talk about. Come on, let's find a place that's more private."

It was so wonderful to hear Yankel's voice, to touch him, to know he survived. We walked away, hand in hand, our hearts filled with love and gratitude. I was euphoric at finding my brother in the same camp as I was—of all places! A tremendous weight lifted from my shoulders. Colors looked brighter and the air smelled fresher. I spent every moment I could with him. My happiness made me feel like a new person.

12

AVRUM

SEPTEMBER 1946 TO MARCH 1947

Finding a Friend

The displaced persons camp or as it was more often called, "the DP center" had, in the beginning, been a mix of all different kinds of refugees. They were of different religions, from big cities to tiny villages, some anxious to return to their country of origin, others swearing to never return to their motherland. Liberated ex-prisoners mingled with former guards—even German soldiers who had taken off their uniforms and melted into the surrounding masses of displaced persons—all mingled together. Everyone in the camps was recognized according to the country he or she was originally from. The American government realized that this was wrong, too dangerous and volatile a mix, and finally separated the Jews from the rest, and put them into their own camps. These camps of Jews immediately flourished. Being in a camp with Jews without the constant, daily threat to my life gave my body and, especially, my mind, a chance to heal. The Jews around me went through the same healing process, which produced a rise in spirit that wanted to give more and receive more. The new camp energy produced everyday activities that had been crushed or eliminated under the Nazi regime.

Plays, music, sports, publications, and other intellectual entertainments blossomed around us.

Now the camp had evolved into a hive of activity. Schools were operating with teachers from America and some from Palestine. The Orthodox Hasidim were also teaching in their own schools. Several different newspapers were available. The communists were busy selling their doctrine. The Zionists were pushing for volunteers to go to Palestine, saying it was the future Jewish homeland. Sports teams from different DP centers competed against each other. Musical groups blossomed and were quite good. There were plays on a regular basis. The different agencies, such as ORT, UNRRA, and the Jewish Agency worked with survivors to prepare them for the future. Chaplains and doctors worked to get people's minds and bodies healthy. The camp population was always in flux, with everyone trying to find his or her way to a new life somewhere. Some of the survivors found recovery relatively simple, while others felt lost and continued to suffer. Most would eventually improve.

Each day, I checked the new lists of the Red Cross and the UNRRA to see if there was anyone I knew on it. I had made a few friends at the camp, but I still had no real direction. Then, one evening I decided to go to a play that had been advertised. I hadn't done anything like that yet, so I looked forward to the new experience. The evening was warm and comfortable as I walked with others to the location of the play. Just as I got there, I thought I saw a familiar face. I jostled my way through the crowd, excited at the possibility of actually connecting with someone from my past. I was shocked to see my friend Yankel with a beautiful girl. "Yankel! Yankel!" I shouted.

He turned, saw me, and froze. His lips formed a silent question: *Avrum?* A look of recognition and shock exploded on his face. His eyes gleamed with excitement as he ran toward me.

I was already running to him, so we slammed into one another. We embraced with joy.

"Avrum," he shouted. "You made it! Oh, how exciting it is to find you here."

"I knew that if anyone could make it, it would be you," I said and motioned to his beautiful companion. "So, is this your girlfriend, or maybe your wife?"

Yankel laughed. "Neither. This is my sister, Mollie. We are so lucky that we found each other. We are the only ones left from our family, but we are still looking every day anyway. And now I've found you! Mollie, this is my friend, Avrum, who I told you about."

I shook her hand for a long time, trying to think of what to say. Her hand felt small and wonderfully soft. I was speechless.

"Hello Avrum," Mollie said. "I am pleased to meet you."

"Me too," I replied, feeling like I'd just heard an angel speak. "I mean I'm pleased to meet you, not meet me."

We all laughed.

Mollie and Me

After that first meeting, I looked for Yankel often, not only because we were friends and I liked him, but also because I was fascinated with Mollie. She was wonderful. Unlike most in the camp, she had worked on a farm during the war and had a striking healthy look that was mesmerizing. There was nothing gaunt, ill, or exhausted about her, which was the standard look at the camp. She was slender but strong, and walked with a confident stride. When she smiled, her rosy cheeks revealed the nicest little dimples and her eyes sparkled. She smiled most of the time. She seemed to enjoy hard work and sometimes had to be told to stop or she would have continued into the night. She was not only self-sufficient, but also supportive and kind. She listened patiently to other people's problems and always had wise suggestions and kind words to say. She was beautiful, which intimidated me terribly. I had no real experience with women, so I often found myself groping for the right thing to say or, sometimes, anything to say. She kept me off balance, though it wasn't on purpose. As we spent more time together, it became easier to talk with her and be myself. I soon came to realize that Mollie had entered my heart and filled it until there was no room for anyone else. It felt wonderful to feel this way about her, but it also hurt. There were so many things I wanted to tell her, romantic things, but I couldn't force the words out of my mouth. I thought I would explode.

I saw how people were connecting all around me. There were several marriages every day between Jews who only weeks before didn't know that one another existed. I sometimes thought these love birds were drunk on freedom and anxious to get on with the rest of their lives, so they put aside formalities and let their emotions do the talking. For me, it was different. I loved Mollie for more reasons than I could explain. I loved everything about her: her looks, her personality, her actions, her philosophy. I couldn't think of one thing about her that I didn't like. But if that one thing ever showed up, I figured I'd probably love that too. I had come to the conclusion that if I wanted a chance to be with Mollie for the rest of my life, I needed to move forward and make my case right away.

I went to Yankel and told him that I needed to speak with him.

"Avrum, you can talk to me any time. What is it that you look so serious about?"

I took a deep breath, then forced out the words. "It's about your sister."

"Is something wrong? You look upset."

"No, no," I stuttered. "Nothing is wrong. That's the problem. Everything is right."

"I don't understand. What does that mean?"

I looked to the heavens for a little help, then looked him in the eyes, and spoke with a dry mouth. "I really like your sister."

His face lit up and a broad smile appeared. "So do I," he said, toying with me.

I was on a roll now and just needed to say what I had to say. "Well, I think I would like to marry her."

"You think?"

"I know. I know I want to marry her."

"Have you told her this?"

I looked at my shoes. "No. Not yet."

He looked hard at me. "Don't you think you ought to talk to Mollie about this?"

"Yes, I know, but how would you feel about such a thing?"

He paused to toy with me, pretending to think for a minute. "I would be pleased to have Mollie marry you, if that is what she wants. I know you are a mensch, a real gentleman. I know I can trust you to do your best for my sister. I would be honored to have you as my brother, but as you know, I intend to find the Jewish Brigade and use their help to make my way to Palestine. I had hoped Mollie might come with me, but I realize how dangerous that will probably be. I don't know for sure what she wants. Even if I can get to Palestine, and if you go to some other place with my sister, I know you will give her a good life and treat her with honor. You'll raise a Jewish family because that for sure is something that's needed."

I listened intently to Yankel, unaware of my jaw hanging open in anticipation of what else he might say.

"You have my blessing, but as I told you, you'd better talk to her. It's her life you're asking for."

I broke out of my trance and grabbed Yankel, giving him a big hug. The smile never left his face. Then, I took a deep breath.

"I'll see you in a while. I have business to take care of."

I turned and took off, anxious to take the all-important next step.

Looking for Mollie

After my conversation with Yankel, I was really excited to find Mollie. My heart beat like that of a running rabbit. I could feel my pulse pounding in my wrists. I had no idea what I would say exactly, but I felt that once I got started, I could get the gist of what I wanted across to her. As I walked with a stride of purpose, it occurred to me that I didn't even know where Mollie's sleeping quarters were, so I went to the camp headquarters. One of the ladies there told me that she could be found at the hospital, where she was helping patients. I asked if it would be okay to go there or if the doctors would not allow my visit. The lady told me that it would be no problem and that I could ask at the desk where to find her once I got there.

I quickly made my way to the hospital area and asked for Mollie. The nurse told me that I could find her in the Social Room, where patients read books and newspapers or, in some cases, played cards or chess. As I entered the room, I saw her, and stopped in place, just inside the doorway. She was in deep conversation with a sad-looking woman. After a moment, she looked up and noticed me, and flashed me a quick, sweet smile. A wave of tingly warmth passed through me. I stood where I was until she ended her conversation, leaned forward and kissed the woman on each cheek. Then she rose and came over to me.

"Avrum, how nice to see you here. Are you okay?"

"Yes, I'm fine, thank you. I came to say hello. They told me I could find you here."

"There's an empty table. Why don't we sit down?"

I was delighted to sit with her and made some small talk. "Mollie, you've told me you work in the hospital, but what exactly do you do here?"

"I'm just a helper. As you know, I was lucky and worked on a Polish farm for most of the war. I was protected from the horrible things that took place at the different camps and workplaces. So now I work with people who have been through unthinkable things, who are scarred by their experiences. Most of them are depressed and do not trust any authority. They feel guilty that they are the only surviving member of a large family. Their health is poor, and they suffer from malnutrition and a variety of different diseases, among other things. My job is to let them talk and get things off their chest and out of their mind, and, hopefully, build a trust. While I'm not trained to do this, I see that I am helping, and any good I can do is a positive step forward."

This was the perfect moment to get to the subject that brought me here. "Do you have any plans beyond this?"

"Not really," she said. "Yankel wants to go to Palestine. He is my only living relative that I am aware of, and he is precious to me. Family means so much, I'm not sure now what I would do if I were separated from him."

"Well, you could marry and raise your own family."

My voice sounded higher than normal, but I felt good now that we were on the subject I wanted to talk about.

She looked up at me, a surprised expression on her face.

"Look around you," I pressed on. "People are getting married every day here. There is a natural need to continue to live and raise a family."

"Yes, that's natural. I've thought about it many times."

"You have?" I nearly tripped over my own tongue.

"Oh, yes. That would be a special, precious thing."

"Mollie, please hear me out. This is important. People here marry after knowing each other for such a short time. Many have very little connection, except that they both want to be free and have a normal life, raising a family."

"Yes, you said that."

"We could be one of those married couples—you and me."

Mollie sat quietly, her eyes round with surprise at my words. I couldn't stop now. But I couldn't manage a smooth, romantic appeal. I'd just empty my heart and hope for the best. "Even though we've known each other for a short time, I have feelings for you. Deep feelings. I think I know you well. I know I love everything about you. I would honor and protect you. You can always trust me to be at your side. There isn't anything I wouldn't do to make you happy."

She just sat there with a soft dimpled smile, her eyes sparkling with emotion. "I already spoke with Yankel and told him about my feelings. He told me to talk to you and that, of course, the decision is all yours. But he smiled as he said it. I know this is out of the blue, but I ask you, Mollie, shall we get married and share the rest of our lives together?"

There was a pause. My thoughts raced. *Oh, my God! I had said it. Would I now explode and cease to exist? Why is she so quiet?*

"Avrum, I need a moment. Please understand: You've made me happy. But I'm overwhelmed. I need to speak with Yankel. Let's meet here in the morning and talk again. I'm afraid I have to get back to work now."

I was both pleased and disappointed as I headed back to my area. I knew it was proper etiquette to ask the woman's father for the hand of his daughter, or in this case, ask the brother for the hand of his sister. It was also common practice and etiquette for the woman to at least talk with a member of her family before making a final decision, but still, as I walked to my quarters, I felt both shaky and exhilarated. I thought to myself, *Well, she didn't say "No!"*

From sunset until the next morning, time felt like it dragged on for weeks. When dawn arrived, the sun rose more brilliantly than I had ever seen. I went to Yankel's area, where Mollie usually joined him to walk to breakfast together. She was already there when I arrived.

As I approached them, I examined their faces, trying to read any clue that things might be in my favor. "Good morning, Yankel! Good morning, Mollie!" I tried to sound calm and happy.

"Yes," Mollie answered.

"Yes, it's a good morning?"

"No," she corrected. "Yes, it's the morning you hoped for."

Every part of me lit up; her words filled me with warmth and excitement.

"Yes," she said, smiling. "*Yes* to your question from yesterday. I talked with Yankel and told him how I have waited all my life for exactly this moment and this person—you."

I threw my arms around her and felt her warm embrace touch me deeply. Yankel put his arms around the two of us and we all cried.

If there was a way to capture this moment and carry it around for the rest of my life, I knew I'd be happy every second of it.

Getting Married

Mollie and I stood with four other couples, all waiting their turn to be married by the US Army chaplain who had been a rabbi in civilian life. To us, he was still a rabbi. He smiled as he looked over the eager couples waiting to be wed. On some days, he married as many as 20 couples. Usually, they stood before him in clothes borrowed for the special event. Each couple, when called, would come forward and stand under the chuppah—a traditional canopy of cloth supported by four poles, representing the home they would build together—to be joined for life according to God's will. Most of the couples hadn't known one another before they came to the displaced persons camp, but they were all driven by a need to find a mate and build a new life.

Love would come later, in many cases. There was a silent understanding between each pair, a realization of how much they needed one another to build a future. A great void within each begged to be filled with companionship and children. These young people who had lost their families would now make families of their own.

I glanced at Mollie and became choked up with pride and love. She looked beautiful! Yankel stood to one side, *kvelling*—the Yiddish word meaning "feeling delighted," or "swelling with pride." He was ready to give his sister away.

Yes, I thought, *I will love and protect her and we, together, will raise a Jewish family.* My mind wandered for a dreamlike moment. *If only my parents and my sister, Lena, could be here too, and be a part of this special event.*

I was suddenly awakened from my trance by the rabbi's voice asking Mollie and me to step forward. My heart raced as we found our places under the chuppa. The rabbi conducted a short-version wedding ceremony and then placed a glass, wrapped in a white napkin, on the floor before us. I stomped on it with a surge of energy and joy. The traditional breaking of the glass symbolized that the marriage would last as long as it would take to reassemble the broken pieces of glass back together. This marriage would definitely last forever.

"I now congratulate Mr. and Mrs. Bielinski on the occasion of their marriage before God and these witnesses," the rabbi decreed.

With that announcement everyone shouted "Mazel tov!" Then Mollie and I kissed, for just a moment, since I felt a little shy showing intimacy in front of others, and we made room for the next couple.

Yankel Leaves

After the wedding, life for Mollie, me, and Yankel became a mixture of routine and spurts of activity. We were already taking measures to get on with our lives. Mollie had her job at the hospital while I tailored for those who needed it and took classes in English. I took to the language quickly and enjoyed trying it out on American soldiers whenever I had the chance. Yankel, while waiting to be contacted to go to Palestine, took classes in Hebrew, in preparation for a future that would require him speaking this language. He stayed alert and a bit on edge, anxious for the opportunity to start his journey to a new life. Mollie and I applied for entry to the United States and then impatiently waited—and prayed—for our application to go through. When we weren't working, the three of us hung out together, attending the social events that were available.

In my spare time, I went to the Red Cross and the Jewish Joint Committee on a regular basis, looking to see if I could get any information on where to find Lena. On one such visit, a Red Cross worker asked me if I knew whether my sister had married.

"I don't know. Why is that important?"

"Well, if she married, then she probably has a new last name."

I felt foolish that I hadn't thought of that at all. I was crushed. I realized that I'd have to go to all the places that I'd already explored and try to find a way to explain that there might be a last name to look for that I didn't even know. The weeks passed, without news, but not without hope and frustration.

One day Mollie asked me if I liked the name David or Daniel. "Which one do you like better?"

"Why does it matter?"

"Well, only because I'm pregnant. We're going to have a baby!"

"Oh, Mollie!" I shouted and, nearly knocking her over, I grabbed her in a big hug, my happiness spilling over. "Let's find Yankel and tell him he's going to be an uncle!"

We found him outside his barracks, with a mysteriously happy look on his face. Had he somehow found out about the precious new addition to our lives?

"Yankel!" I got his attention. "We've got great news!"

"Hey, Avrum, Mollie! I've got news too."

"You're going to be an uncle!" Mollie announced.

"Uncle Yankel," I added.

"God in heaven!" he crowed. "That is amazing news. You wasted no time making a Jewish family. What a blessing!"

"What is *your* news?" I asked.

"I've just learned that the Jewish Brigade will take a group to Palestine. They've picked names from a list of Jews who want to go and I am included in the group!"

"Oh, what wonderful news!" Mollie said, tears welling up in her eyes. "We're all blessed with the best news possible."

"Yes, the very best, but my news must remain secret. The trip will not be very legal, if you know what I mean," he added in a hushed tone and a mischievous smirk.

"When will this happen?" I asked.

"I think in the next day or two. I'm told a Jewish Brigade truck will pass through and collect our group, then we'll go to a seaport in Italy, and then to Palestine." Yankel paused for a moment, then he put his hand on my shoulder. "I'm sad to leave you both, but I know my sister is in good hands."

We said goodnight to one another, as we hugged and cried. Each of us was looking forward to an unknown, yet bright future.

Two nights later, three Jewish Brigade trucks pulled into the camp, each carrying Jewish refugees in the back. The officer in charge of the convoy told the camp officer that they were transferring their passengers to a different camp, a necessary lie that was easily accepted. He certainly couldn't say he was smuggling Jews to Palestine and since no refugees could be moved without some sort of politically acceptable reason, he used his rank to okay the movement of the group. The Brigade officer added that they'd eat something in camp before they left. The camp officer waved them through the gate.

The convoy wound its way through the camp and stopped at a predetermined spot where Yankel and three other people climbed into the third truck. There were already five other people stowed in the back. Upon seeing them, Yankel introduced himself, as did everyone else. The last to introduce themselves was a young couple. "My name is Solomon, but everyone calls me Sol. This is my wife, Anna. We're pleased to be here together with all of you."

With a rumble of engines, the trucks pulled out and started the first leg of the journey to Palestine.

To America

Mollie and I were happy that Yankel was living his dream, but we missed him very much. We had been a threesome for a few months and had thoroughly enjoyed it. Being together was positive therapy for us all. We shared our dreams and thoughts, laughed and cried, supported and loved one another.

My activities intensified as I checked daily with UNRRA, Red Cross, and the Jewish Joint Committee to see if I could find Lena or any of my relatives. I had found the names of some of my father's and mother's relatives, all of which had perished in the death camps. I was happy that my sister's name didn't appear on any of those kinds of lists. There was hope. I knew in my heart that she was alive. I would keep on looking for her.

Then Mollie and I received great news. We were included on the list of immigrants to be accepted to the United States. We were part of the quota that would go on the next ship to our future home. President Harry Truman had used enormous political pressure to reverse national policy. With the information he received from Earl G. Harrison, his special representative, he managed to get an affirmative vote of the United States Congress to make it possible for many displaced persons to go to the US. We were ecstatic. A caseworker told us to be in the main yard in two days, where we would be picked up and taken to the port of Bremerhaven. During those two days, we collected our few belongings and prepared ourselves for the journey of our dreams.

When we reached the ship, they loaded us alphabetically and told us where our quarters would be for the voyage. Mollie and I were separated, as were all the married couples. The women were quartered in the bow and the men in the stern of the ship. We were to cross the ocean on the USS Sturgis, which had previously been used as a US troop ship, but had now been refitted to shuttle displaced persons to their destinations. We were told that we would be at sea for about two weeks. When we asked about what part of the United States we were sailing to, a crew member told us "New Orleans." We all looked at each other, as if he'd spoken in an unknown foreign language. Was that close to New York? Or San Francisco?

We would soon find out.

The Voyage

The sleeping quarters were very tight, both the men's and the women's. Privacy hardly existed. I met two new friends who, though from different countries, had been traveling together for some time. Velvel was from Lithuania and Yuri from the Ukrainian area of Russia. We mostly communicated in Yiddish, although we tried to use English, since we were going to America. Yuri's English was not so bad, but Velvel struggled with the language. After a few words in English, he usually reverted back to Yiddish. Yuri had been in a couple of German satellite work camps during the war and had learned a bit of English because of the various nationalities of the prisoners. Velvel had fought with the Russian partisans even though he had no desire to be a communist. Of course, he never told this to his commanding officers. No one spoke a word of English among the partisans and so Velvel had no opportunity—and no interest—to hear anyone speak it. I would change that. I made sure that we held most of our conversations in English to help my two friends along. I also spoke English with Mollie most of the time, so we would be properly prepared for life in America.

The first evening at sea, Velvel told Yuri that he thought this was a nice boat.

"This is a ship, not a boat."

"Who told you this is not a boat?"

"A sailor told me."

"Then what is a boat?"

"A boat is what you get into when the ship sinks. That's what a boat is," Yuri explained in a raised, frustrated voice.

"Who cares? A boat, a ship, whatever, as long as it takes us to go wherever we want to go."

It was hard not to laugh at these two.

Earlier in the evening, I had dinner with Mollie. We had to eat standing up, with our food on a raised table. It was a little awkward because of the rolling ocean waves and the swaying motion of the ship, but we managed. It was as though we were mastering a new sort of dance. The three of us—Mollie, me, and our baby-to-be—were happy to be going to a promising destination.

The next morning the weather got blustery, and the ship pitched and swayed as it cut its way through the angry waves. Almost everyone got sick and vomited wherever they were, creating an awful stench that made everyone even sicker. I made my way up to the deck to get some fresh air and—with a little luck—find Mollie. After 20 minutes of searching, I finally found her, standing on the deck, gripping the railing. She was as white as a ghost.

"Avrum, I feel terrible. My stomach feels awful. This won't harm the baby, will it?"

I assured her that it wouldn't, without really knowing. My medical knowledge was limited to wives' tales and ancient remedies that were passed down from generation to generation. I told her later, when we went to lunch, that she should try and eat crackers and bread. Only then did I realize that talking about food made her even more miserable and didn't help me either.

We suffered through four days of turbulent weather and then, as quickly as the storm arrived, it disappeared. The dark gray clouds melted away, the ocean smoothed out, and everyone came on deck to enjoy the smell of the sea and soak up the warm sun. I was counting the days. Only another nine to ten days and we would reach land. I hoped there were no more storms in front of us.

Many people on deck passed the time by playing cards and chess, while others played checkers with the competitive spirit and ferocity of sword fighters. Most of us had adjusted to the rolling ship and were now able to keep food down. We were all feeling much better and more optimistic. We had a lot of time to reflect. I sat on deck and thought about Momma and Poppa. I could hear Momma singing "Little Child, Little Child" as if she stood there before me. I also thought of Lena. She was a child when she left and now she would be a young woman. I tried to imagine my little sister that way but found it difficult. I was anxious to get to America, get situated, and resume my search for her.

Yuri and Velvel roused me out of my thoughts. "Where is Mollie?" Velvel asked.

"Oh, she's talking with some friends about the best way to have a baby."

He thought a moment, looking confused. "There's more than one way?"

"If they're talking about it, then I guess there must be."

"Avrum," Yuri broke in. "Do you think that people in the United States know what happened to the Jews in Europe? Do you think they know what the Germans did? Do you think they know about the crematoriums and the death camps?"

"Just a minute," I said, holding up my hands. "I'm sure they know. I saw the reactions on the faces of the American soldiers, and I believe they will go back to their homes and tell their families about what they saw."

My friends stared at me as they thought over what I'd just said.

"But I'll tell you this," I continued. "I will learn English well enough to go to meetings and tell everyone who will listen about what happened. My friends, I ask you, why did we survive when others did not?"

They all shook their heads.

"Exactly! I don't know why either, but I do know that it is our duty to bear witness and not let anyone forget this terrible tragedy. We need to stand tall and show them that we are proud to be Jews."

"Yes," Velvel said.

"Absolutely!" Yuri agreed vehemently.

The conversation ended on an emotional note., We fell into thought, each of us processing my ideas in his own, personal way.

I think we all felt a new conviction about what we needed to do to never let the horrors we suffered happen again. We hugged each other, happy with the understanding we shared between us.

The days passed one after the other. We were mostly in good spirits, thanks to the good weather—an answer to our prayers. The ship's passengers had eaten good food and were well-rested. Their improved health was obvious, judging from the pink cheeks and big smiles I saw everywhere. Then, one day the ship's officer made an announcement over the speakers.

"Attention all passengers! Tomorrow we reach the port of New Orleans. Please be ready to disembark at 8 a.m."

The announcement was short, but the excitement was absolutely electric. Mollie and I looked at each other with love and a deep understanding that we were now about to set foot into our future, to actually walk into it and feel it. It was hard to sleep that night. A million thoughts ran through our minds. We'd soon be in a place without the sight of destroyed buildings and the rubble of war. Streets would be clear and open. There would be stores with food and clothing. People would probably be wearing clean clothes, not rags. Would tomorrow ever arrive?

Everyone was up early the next morning, so early that it was too dark to see the mainland. Then, one of the most remarkable experiences of my life took place. With Mollie in my arms, I watched the darkness lift and disappear, and there in front of us lay the United States of America. With tears in our eyes, we all thanked God.

America

We were thrilled as we started unloading onto the solid ground of the United States. There was activity everywhere. Various organizations had members there to help passengers figure out where they should go next. Relatives of passengers held up signs with names on them and shouted the name of whomever they'd come to meet. Immigration officers sat at desks inside a few buildings, while others guided passengers to the proper places. All the immigrants were being met at the gangplank by female members of the Port and Dock Committee of the Service to the Foreign-born Program, which was sponsored by the Council of Jewish Women. Their mission was to help the passengers socialize and integrate into the local communities. Most of the immigrants were moving on to other destinations.

The first task was to sort out the passengers in alphabetical order.

Instructions were shouted in several languages. Mollie and I went to a table for all those whose names started with the letter "b". Mollie nudged me and pointed to two women who were waving a sign with Bielinski painted on it.

I grabbed Mollie's hand and waved at them. "Here! Here! We are Bielinski!"

They came over and with broad smiles introduced themselves. "I'm Ruthie Cohen and this is my friend Judy Greenberg. We're here to help you get settled. Do you speak English?"

"Yes, we do!" I proudly said with as little accent as I could muster. I was thrilled to hear English being spoken to me, not as a way to practice, but as a real language being used every day. I could understand them, which relieved me enormously. Better yet, they could understand me.

"We can speak Yiddish, if that's easier," Ruthie offered.

"Let's give English a try," I suggested.

"Yes, that's a good idea," Mollie said, giving me a coy smile. These were her very first words to someone who grew up speaking English. I could see how pleased she was.

"Follow us," Ruthie said.

Just then, a young woman came running up to us, calling out Mollie's name. The lady had seen the sign showing our name and followed it. We stopped and waited as she approached us. Out of breath, she turned to Ruthie. "I'm sorry I'm late," she apologized. "I'm their sponsor. I was contacted by the Jewish Agency when they were overseas. The Agency told me that because they applied for papers to come here, they needed a sponsor. So, the Agency found my family. I'm a cousin."

Mollie's eyes widened in disbelief. "A cousin? Family?"

"My name is Wendy Resnick. I live in Cleveland. My mother is Mollie's mother's sister."

"Oh God!" Mollie said and broke into tears. The two cousins hugged each other and then, under the supervision of Ruthie and Judy, we gathered the few things we had and followed them.

The five of us left the processing building and got into two cars out front. From there, we drove through a busy downtown and finally to our destination in a residential area: a small apartment in a fourplex. It consisted of two small bedrooms, a living room, bathroom, and kitchen. It was old but looked like a palace to us. Ruthie told us to leave our things at the apartment, because we needed to go get groceries. The five of us got into Ruthie's car—a 'station wagon,' they said—and we went to a place called Safeway, a store that was filled with things to eat and drink and was as large as a small village. I was shocked when we walked in, my mind spinning. *So much food and so many choices!*

I asked Ruthie, "How shall we choose? How much money do we have to spend?"

She smiled and started to say something, but in my excitement, I interrupted. "Can we buy two oranges, one for Mollie and one for me?"

Mollie jumped in enthusiastically. "If we cut them in half, we can have them for two days."

"Why don't you buy a dozen?" Ruthie suggested. "You can if you want, you know."

My mind tried to digest the idea. *Imagine. We could buy a dozen oranges. One for every day of the week, with five left over.*

I smiled and nodded. Mollie and I followed the three women as they shopped for us, asking about what sorts of things we wanted, making suggestions, and putting whatever we bought into what they called "a shopping cart." Mollie and I were eager students, hungry to learn this way of buying things. When we got back to our new home, Ruthie and Judy told us they would come back the next day and take me to a job interview they had arranged. They left, but Wendy stayed with us to help us put away the groceries. Then she left as well, saying she would return the following day. The door closed, and Mollie and I sat down to absorb everything that happened this momentous day. We were by ourselves now. Our new life in America was a reality.

Being Americans

The next day Ruthie and Judy picked me up to take me to the job interview. My clothes were not as perfect as I would have liked to apply for a job, but they were all I had. The second-hand European-style suit that I'd gotten in the DP camp looked unpressed and a bit saggy. I hoped it wouldn't make a bad impression at the interview. We went to a place called "Regal Clothiers" and waited in the foyer for Mr. Steiner, the owner. Ruthie and Judy left for a while and said they would come back and get me. I was ushered into Mr. Steiner's office. He was a pleasant-looking man and asked me to be seated.

"Avrum," he said, "my name is Ziggy Steiner. I'm the owner of this company. We make different kinds of ready-made shirts. I am told you are a tailor. Is that true?"

I cleared my throat. "Yes Mr. Steiner, I am. And a good one too. I learned from my father, who was also a tailor—"

"Please call me Ziggy. Everyone calls me that."

"Yes, Mr. Ziggy, I will do that."

He chuckled. "I understand you are a survivor of the death camps. Life, I assure you, will be better here. I have a few employees like you who are also from the camps. We work five-day weeks here. I pay on the 1st and 15th of the month. We take off all national holidays, and I close for the Jewish holidays of Rosh Hashanah and Yom Kippur. Your supervisor will be Mrs. Glaberman. Do you have any questions?"

I shook my head No. Then we talked for a short while. He told me his family had come to America from Germany at the turn of the century. He said there were a lot of German Jews in the area at that time. He asked about Mollie, and we chatted a bit. He made me feel comfortable. Then he gave me a big smile and ended the interview. "You start on Monday."

His words surprised me. *That was it? My God, I have a job! That fast.* We shook hands and I left his office, elated. Ruthie and Judy were waiting outside to take me home. I was overjoyed and couldn't wait to get home and tell Mollie. As we were driving, Ruthie asked if there was anything else she could do for me. I told her about Lena and asked if there was a place here where someone could help me find her. She said she would let me know. When I got home, Mollie and Wendy were cleaning the apartment. I told them what had happened at Regal Clothiers. Mollie was thrilled at the good news. She asked how much I was getting paid.

"Oy Mollie, I forgot to ask."

We all laughed.

Wendy left the next day to go back home to Cleveland, leaving Mollie and me to figure out life in America on our own. I continually worked hard on improving my English. So many things were different from Poland here. Mollie and I had never seen such and amazing mix of peoples here. Americans were proud of their diversity. Imagine. A country made up of people of all nations, all religions, all colors living together. Here in New Orleans there's a large group of people called Cajuns, who were known for their spicy food. Since we lived close the Gulf of Mexico, there was a lot of seafood available. We joined a small synagogue and met new people. Then, the event we'd been waiting for—the one that would change our lives forever—took place: Mollie gave birth to a healthy baby boy in a beautiful, clean hospital. We called him Joshua Rueben: "Joshua" for my grandfather and "Rueben" for Mollie's grandfather. Our new son gave me even greater reason and energy to do well in America, to make something of myself and provide well for my family. The Bielinski name would continue on.

The following months were all about learning and adjusting. I loved my job and the people I worked with. I was one of many tailors employed here, sitting at a modern sewing machine and putting shirts together. We were part of a larger number of specialists in the building, including cutters, pressers, and everyone involved in manufacturing shirts. My attention to detail and quality were noticed and earned me increasingly better opportunities. I got a few raises in salary and was promoted a few times until I was given the job of supervisor. I got along quite well with everyone and my style of dealing with the workers seemed to create a happy and productive atmosphere. It was a good life.

One day, Mr. Ziggy's secretary came to tell me that he wanted to see me in his office. I stood at the open door of his office and knocked on the door jamb. "Come in, sit down," his voice boomed.

As I sat down, he went on.

"I've been watching you. You work so well with the tailors, and you get things done. You're doing really well. I especially like that everyone enjoys being around you and that you seem to inspire everyone you talk to. I have an opportunity for you if you are interested. I've noticed how much your English has improved. Regal needs a salesman to go out and sell our shirts in the rural areas. Even though you're an excellent tailor, I think you'd bring more value to the company as a salesman. Do you think you could do that? Are you interested in being a salesman? You would get a raise and a car to get you where you need to go. What do you think?"

"I think yes, but of course I must ask my wife. Can I give you an answer tomorrow?"

"Absolutely. I'll see you tomorrow."

I couldn't wait to get home and tell Mollie. I charged into our apartment and let her know the news.

"How much is the raise?" she asked.

I forgot to ask, again. What was it with me and money?

"My news might not be as amazing as yours."

"You have news?"

"I certainly do. I'm pregnant again."

Oy vey! How much joy could one day hold? What a happy day!

We Settle In

Mr. Ziggy prepared me for my future as a salesman. He had business cards made for me and put my name down as "Avi"—no last name—and bought a used station wagon for me. He told me I would take enough merchandise with me so I could deliver the shirts as I sold them. When I got the car, I immediately practiced driving, since I had little experience. One small problem, though: I needed a driver's license. So, I studied the driver's manual and, with some help from fellow employees, I passed the driver's test and was now legal. Mollie and I were excited about this big step up in the world. I felt a buoyant sense of freedom and a power over the destiny of me and my family. I could put them in the car and go anywhere we wished. Mr. Ziggy and I worked out a route for me to take and I motored off on my new adventure.

I pulled up to my first potential customer at a rundown-looking general store in a small town. When I walked into the store, I couldn't believe the chaotic amount of merchandise strewn about. I asked a young boy who was putting tags on clothing where I could find the owner. Before he could answer, an older woman stepped out from behind some flour sacks and informed me that she was the boss. I smiled and proudly handed her my business card. "I am Avrum Bielinski from Regal Clothiers. May I ask your name?"

"Ida Mae Slocum, but just call me Ida Mae. I own this place. What are you selling?"

"Shirts. Ready-made shirts. Look, here they are." I opened my small suitcase of inventory. "Beautiful quality and very nice material."

"How much are they?"

I told her the prices, whereupon she informed me that her customers wouldn't pay that much when they could make a shirt for a lot less. I tried to convince her that this was a good deal, but she was quite adamant. "I'll tell you what, how about if I leave you six shirts: two styles in three sizes. When I come back on my next visit, I'll take back whatever you haven't sold if you want me to. That way there is no risk."

She thought about that for a minute and agreed. I hoped Mr. Ziggy would be okay with what I did, but I had a good feeling about it. Ida Mae studied me a long moment and finally asked a question. "Where are you from?"

I thought for a minute and said that I was from Germany, because that's where our ship had departed from. She gave me a look of amused disbelief and informed me that a lot of German people lived in the area, and none sounded like me. I chuckled and explained that I had lived in Germany, but I wasn't German, and so that's where I was from, but not where I was born. The explanation was good enough for her.

That was the beginning of my sales career. I used the same logic with other customers, offering to leave a number of shirts that they could return if unable to sell them. I did quite well, and Mr. Ziggy was very pleased. Time passed quickly and it seemed like a snap of the fingers before Mollie and I had three children: two boys and a little girl. One day Mollie told me she wanted to talk to me about a serious subject.

"Yes, what is it?"

"I've been thinking that it would be nice to move to Cleveland, where cousin Wendy and the rest of my family lives."

I had to sit down. "Why, Mollie? What's wrong with here, where I have a good job and we're settled in?"

"You know that I don't enjoy the hot, humid weather here and there are many more Polish Jews in Cleveland. Even after so many years here, I think I would be more comfortable living close to family and a synagogue and atmosphere that's more like the way I grew up. I know you would have to get a new job, but will you think about it?"

I said I would. I gave it a great deal of thought and decided to discuss Mollie's request with Mr. Ziggy. He was fair and honest, and I was interested in his opinion. He always put others first, so I knew he'd tell me what he thought was best for me. I felt insensitive when I saw the pained look on his face as I told him what Mollie and I had discussed.

He lit a cigarette and said, "Avrum, you've been a special employee here and you are also a good friend. I would be sorry to lose you, but it's important that you have a happy wife and a happy home. Why don't you give it more thought, discuss it with your wife, and let me know your decision in a couple days. If you decide to move, I have a relative who lives in Shaker Heights, which is a suburb of Cleveland. He is in the textile business, and I can arrange a meeting between the two of you."

And so, my family and I moved to Cleveland, Ohio.

13

COMING TOGETHER
MAY 1947 TO JULY 1947

To Palestine

The three Jewish Brigade trucks traveled through the night over paved and dirt roads. In the morning they stopped at a small village, a welcome break for all the travelers. It had been prearranged that they would be given breakfast at the village, as well as some food to take with them. The drivers told their passengers that they still had a full day of travel before they would arrive at their destination. The journey continued on with only a single toilet break along the way until, finally, they stopped in a wooded area where the passengers were told to get out of the trucks. They were met by two young Palestinians, who had been waiting for them, a man and a woman.

The head Jewish Brigade driver informed the passengers. "This is as far as we can go. We must return with the trucks, but you are in good hands. These people are from B'riha, an underground Jewish organization that helps Jewish Holocaust survivors start new lives in Palestine. B'riha means "escape" in Hebrew, and that's what they will help you do. They will help you escape the past and lead you to your future, to your final destination. They'll take you to a seaport where a ship is waiting to bring you to Palestine. God bless you all and good luck on your travels."

The drivers and the two young people from B'riha shook hands and the trucks left. The two Palestinians stepped forward. The leader, Yossi, introduced himself and his companion, Esther.

"If you have any questions at any time, just ask and we will do our best to answer them. We will be a small group. There will be the 50 of you and we have another 175 refugees waiting for us down the trail. It will be a long walk to the ship, about two days. We have people of all ages here, so it's important that we help each other. We'll be walking through some forest and mountain passes with snow and places where there are no roads. Be assured, we know the way."

Yossi asked if there was anyone here who had experience with traveling in a forest. The group looked at one another, wondering who might raise their hand. Sol took Anna's hand and the two stepped forward.

"My wife and I do. We were partisans in the Parczew forest in Poland. We'll do whatever you ask from us."

"Good!" Let's get started. We'll meet the rest of our party down the trail."

After a 20-minute walk, they came to the edge of what looked like a large forest. Yossi brought the group to a stop, pulled a bright blue handkerchief from his pocket, and waved it vigorously in the air. A few moments later, a young man stepped out from behind one of the trees with a big smile on his face.

"Hello Yossi!" the man yelled.

"Hello Shimon, are you ready?"

"Let's go! Come out and let's get moving," Shimon yelled at the forest.

Almost like an illusion, a large group of people quietly appeared from behind the trees. They were a mix of young and old, single people and families with children holding onto their parents' hands. Yossi led the combined groups onto a path leading towards their destination with Esther in the middle and Shimon in the rear. Yossi had asked Sol and Anna to watch over the people and give help to those who might be struggling. Some of the travelers wore newer clothes, while others still wore older, thread-bare clothes left over from where they had come from. Money for food, some clothes, and the necessary bribes had been donated by American sources.

The first night the group stopped in a small village that was prepared to receive them. They had a warm meal and slept in the soft hay of village barns. They were given food to take with them on the trip by some villagers who were very cooperative (and very well paid). This would be the last village they would encounter on their trip. The next morning at daybreak, the combined group started out. The beginning of the trail was tough and it got even more difficult as they gradually climbed to higher altitudes, where the air became thin. The group had to stop often, especially to accommodate the older people.

Yankel saw a mother carrying one child and holding the hand of another. He went over to the young mother and asked if he could help. She looked instantly relieved.

"Thank you. It would be a Godsend. This is my daughter Mollie."

"That's a beautiful name. In fact, I have a sister named Mollie." Yankel bent over and addressed the little girl. "How old are you, Mollie?"

"I'm eight years old," she said in a shy little voice.

"Come take my hand, and we'll help each other walk."

The group moved on until they came to patches of white sparkling snow lying thin upon the ground. Looking ahead, farther up the mountain, they could see even larger patches, much closer together. Though the air was cold and crisp, and required short breaths to keep their chests from hurting, no one complained. They trudged on until nightfall, when they found an ideal area that offered protection from the wind. Yossi made a hand gesture for everyone to stand in place, which they gratefully did. The group was exhausted and happy to stop. Sol and Anna sprang into action, helping everyone find branches and parts of fallen trees to use as fuel to build fires for warmth. Yossi told everyone that the next day they would start down the mountain and before the end of the day would reach their destination. With this in mind, the group settled in. They covered themselves with the wool blankets brought for the journey and did their best to have a good night's sleep.

The Ship

The column of marchers walked down the long incline on their heels in order to keep their balance. Those having difficulties were helped by others, which allowed the entire group to move at a fairly decent pace. The path was steep, but the trail felt soft. They walked on fallen pine needles that had compressed into a spongy carpet over the seasons. Yossi encouraged the group to keep moving, telling them that they were getting close to their destination and would reach their final goal in no time. The thought of living in a free land without the worries of intimidation was enough to energize those who were exhausted from the long march. It was difficult, but no one complained.

Morning turned into noon, and the group stopped briefly for a lunch of bread, salted meat, and an apple for each. Afterwards, they moved on, everyone feeling better from the rest and food. As they rounded a corner on a steep, winding mountain path, one of the marchers in front shouted, "Water! There's water!"

Everyone moved faster to take a look. The entire group stood like statues, hypnotized by the panoramic scene. There before them sprawled the Mediterranean Sea, its breathtaking blue waters glimmering and shining in the afternoon sunlight. The weary group felt choked with emotion, their teary eyes awed by the sight and the realization that they were about to complete yet another step in their quest toward reaching the Promised Land.

Bolstered with new energy, Yossi and his team led the marchers down the final incline of the mountain to the edge of town. They then skirted around the outer boundary of the town until they reached some docks where a group of young people were waiting. One of the young men in the group shouted out, "Yossi! Shalom, Yossi!"

"Shalom, Nathan! Here we are! We are ready!"

The idea of being ready to sail sent a shiver through the band of travelers. Yankel bent down on one knee and softly said to little Mollie, "Do you know what 'shalom' means?"

She shook her head.

"It's the greeting that is used by the Jews in Palestine when they say hello and also goodbye. In Hebrew, it means "peace." Isn't that a beautiful way to greet someone?"

Mollie smiled and nodded.

The young men led all the refugees onto the dock, where they organized them into smaller groups and gave them numbers. All the time they were given information and directions, they couldn't take their eyes off the ship that was being prepared to take them to Palestine. They watched young Jewish Palestinians finishing the building of toilets on the main deck. Below the deck they had created rows of platform shelves to be used as sleeping racks. The space was very tight but would accommodate many more people than the ship normally carried. Supplies were being loaded by large cranes onto the decks, where they were lashed into place in case the ship met rough waters. Yossi told our group of travelers to stay in the area around the docks and get some rest. They were given bags of food and settled down, happy to not have to walk any farther. No one knew exactly when the ship would depart, but they figured that they'd learn more about the schedule soon.

A shrill train whistle interrupted the early evening quiet. Everyone looked up to see a train slowly chugging around the outskirts of the town, its black smoke billowing out of the engine. The train pulled up to the dock and the young Palestinians ran toward it, to make ready for its arrival. With a great hiss and explosion of steam, it came to a stop and about 1,500 refugees spilled out of the long line of train cars, guided by another group of young Palestinians, who helped to transfer them directly onto the ship. The train passengers were a mix of refugees from Eastern Europe: Poland, Hungary, Romania, Ukraine, Russia, Latvia, Lithuania, and Germany. They, like Yossi's group, were comprised of all ages of men and women in various conditions of health. They had gotten onto the train at various stops along their journey with this ship designated as their final destination. On their trip, though they had been schooled to communicate in Hebrew, they quickly found that everyone could communicate in Yiddish, and another word of Hebrew wasn't spoken. The ship's crew was all-Greek, except for three Americans: the captain, a chief engineer and a doctor.

Yankel wondered how everyone would all fit on this steamer, even if it was a big ship. He mentioned it to Yossi, who laughed. "Wait until you meet the 350 passengers already on the ship. They've been waiting for four days for our arrival."

Yankel's eyes widened. He was speechless. *Could the ship hold around 2,000 people? This will be an interesting journey*, he thought. *I don't think anyone will feel cold with so many people crowded together.*

Also on board, help was provided by a small team of about 30 members of Mossad Le'Aliya B, a well-trained military team from the Palestinian Palmach Marine unit. It was their duty to organize and direct the approximate 2,000 refugees and help in any way necessary.

The refugees all continued boarding the ship and were shown to their crowded quarters, group by group, until everyone was aboard. Then, a nautical bell rang, and the ship slowly pulled away from the dock under a cloak of darkness. They sailed at night to avoid any British naval vessels that might try to prevent the voyage. Yankel was awed by the sight of so many Jews in one place, so full of hope, on their way to achieve a common goal of freedom and new life in Palestine.

Sailing to the Promised Land

The old, refitted steamer was far out at sea when the light of dawn awoke its passengers. Refugees, guides, and military personnel were crammed into every possible space aboard the floating relic. The 4,000-ton cargo ship had been rescued from a journey to the scrap heap by the Haganah, the Jewish armed force in Palestine that was sponsoring the trip. The cost had been high to build scaffolding and sleeping accommodations, create an infirmary, and feed all the passengers, but the vision of the Jewish leadership in Palestine was to bring as many Jews as they could to populate the British protectorate while they advocated for a Jewish homeland. The ship churned through the temperate Mediterranean waters under the power of an old up-and-down coal-fired engine that had a maximum speed of approximately five knots (just under 9.7 kilometers per hour) in good weather. The Palmach Marines were all nautically trained, so in case of an emergency they could operate the steamer.

The first day at sea brought unexpected surprises. Yankel ran into Sol and Anna on deck, who he had traveled together with in the back of the Jewish Brigade truck at Feldafing. They were happy to find each other again. They also met a refugee from Poland named Mendel, who turned out to be a very interesting man. Yankel and Mendel had shared similar experiences. Both had been in Dachau and Auschwitz. The four of them discussed what their hopes and plans were when they would finally arrive in Palestine. They talked endlessly, played chess and cards, reminisced about days gone by, and always kept a constant lookout for the appearance of a British plane or naval vessel.

The Palmach Marines were led by Nathan Siegel, a native of Port City of Haifa. His expertise on the area, and especially the waters on the way to and surrounding Palestine was vitally important. He held a meeting on the third day at sea. He asked the American captain to join the meeting. Anything that happens on a ship must include the captain, who's responsible for the welfare and safety of all. Nathan told the group that he had bad news.

"I'm sure I saw a British cutter tailing us, slipping in and out of sight. We're getting very close to Haifa now, but I really don't think we can make it."

"What can we do?" the captain asked.

"I have a plan. I want to get some of the passengers to land without the British realizing it. We can't help everyone, but we can get some of them to Palestine."

"How will you do that?"

"First, I believe we should identify those passengers who we think can be good soldiers and fighters. Then, around midnight, when the ship is quiet and the British can't see what we're doing, we'll put 20 of them into each of two lifeboats and send them to our destination in Palestine, where the Haganah will be waiting for them. With the motors on the lifeboats, they'll be much faster than this whale of a ship. We'll be about 15 nautical miles from land at that point and still in international waters. I don't believe the British cutter is close enough to see us launch the lifeboats since we haven't seen them, except for my one sighting, and it will be at night, with enough cloud cover to make visibility impossible."

"What if the British decide to stop us at night?" the captain asked.

"We have a history of stoppages that are in our favor. The British seem to like to do them in daylight, when they can see what they're doing."

"What if they decide to close the distance to us and stay near us until morning?" the captain persisted.

"As soon as we drop the lifeboats, we'll head south, along the coast toward Tel Aviv. We'll keep our lights on, to attract attention while the lifeboats move in darkness. The British cutter should keep us in sight at night by following our lights. Even if they close the distance to us, we'll be far removed from the lifeboats. There's no doubt we'll be caught the next day when it's light enough. We'll be taken to Cyprus for detention, but I'm not worried about that, because we will escape the detention camp."

A chuckle ran through the Marines, some of whom had already escaped detention camp more than once. Nathan asked if there were any objections to his plan. The Marines shook their heads.

"Good, then. Hopefully, we will have bought enough time for the lifeboats to make it to land before the British could catch up to us. Now we need to identify the 40 people who we will put in the lifeboats. We will also explain to them how important it is that they keep silent about our plan."

Nathan, the captain, and the ship's American doctor went through the list of passengers on the ship, pooling their individual memories of those aboard. The doctor had been extremely busy checking out the health of everyone on the ship and was able to add his opinion to the selection process. Settling on 40 individuals seemed like an impossible task, but after several hours of intense work, the list was boiled down to 65 prime candidates. In another hour, they finally arrived at the 40 names.

The Marines immediately went through the ship to find the people whose names were on the list and bring them to a stateroom that could accommodate a meeting of that size. Each candidate was told to bring his or her belongings and papers, if they had any. After being briefed on what was expected of them, they went to the lifeboats, where they waited for the next step. By this time, midnight was only a few minutes away. The plan went smoothly as the designated refugees made their way to the lifeboats. Sol, Anna, Yankel, and Mendel were among those chosen to go ashore.

Quietly, the lifeboats were lowered into the calm water and the refugees climbed down on rope ladders. When they got comfortably situated in the boats, they started the motors and headed off toward land. They were immediately swallowed by the darkness.

The two boats moved fast, cutting easily through the water, the whiteness of their wake disappearing and blending into the quiet Mediterranean. It wasn't long before they spotted land, and soon after made it to the sandy beach rendezvous point. The boats pulled up onto the sand, where they were met by Jewish soldiers in khakis who took the travelers to two trucks.

For the refugees who got out of the lifeboats, putting their feet on the holy soil of Palestine was exhilarating. A few dropped to their knees and put their foreheads against wet sand, mumbling prayers of thanks to God. The refugees were loaded onto the two trucks, and immediately took off, one headed south and the other north. Sol and Anna found themselves in the truck going south while Yankel and Mendel went in the northbound truck. The plan to get some refugees safely to the shore had worked.

The next day, just after the first light of morning, a British observation plane flew over the steamer, rounded the ship, and then disappeared into the horizon. Later in the day, Nathan observed two British cutters following the laboring steamer, moving ever closer at maximum speed. He went to the bridge, where the captain stood at the helm, looking over the instruments. The captain gave a nod and a wink to Nathan, who returned the gestures, and added a smile. Next destination: Cyprus.

The Promised Land

Sol, Anna, Yankel, and Mendel sped along to their separate destinations in the territory of Palestine. They were thrilled to be there but had no idea of the turmoil that consumed the area. The Yashuv, the Jewish community in Palestine, had been working hard politically—and covertly—to form the structure of a Jewish state-to-be. The Palestinian Arabs, with the help of their British overlords, were trying to crush any hope of the Yashuv turning Palestine into a Jewish homeland. The Grand Mufti of Jerusalem, Hajj Amin Al-Huayni, who admired the Nazis and hated the Jews, did everything he could to spread his poisonous propaganda to the Arab residents of Palestine.

Continual clashes between Arabs and Jews added to the state of unrest throughout the territory. Each group wanted its own statehood. The Jews were willing to coexist with an Arab neighbor state, but the Arabs were not willing to coexist with a Jewish homeland. So, while the Jews accepted a proposal by the United Nations for a Jewish state next to an Arab state, the Arabs turned it down.

Sol and Anna, along with their fellow travelers from the ship, were taken to a small kibbutz in the south: Yad Mordechai. Founded in 1930, the kibbutz had been built on a hill and dominated the coastal highway between Gaza and Ashkelon. All traffic along the coast in this area had to pass by the kibbutz.

The refugees were received with a happy welcome by a reception team from the kibbutz, who immediately fed the weary travelers. Afterwards, they were issued clean clothes and shown to their living quarters. Then, the travelers were brought to a meeting room where they were questioned by the kibbutz leaders. Each refugee was asked the same four questions: Where were you born? Where did you spend the last five years? Have you had any military experience? And how well can you speak and understand Hebrew?

After their interviews, the group was given their responsibilities and handed over to experienced residents who would help them with what needed to be done. Anna and Sol were delighted. This experience was a dramatic transition from what they had known in their young lives. They were introduced to new foods, such as dates, guava, pomegranates, falafel, and shawarma. They were thrilled to be surrounded by fellow Jews.

In the north, Yankel and Mendel were taken to a kibbutz called Mishmar Ha'Emek, located in the western Jezreel Valley. The kibbutz housed a little over 500 residents. It had previously been used by the British as a training facility. But now it was continually harassed by bands of armed terrorists from nearby Arab villages, which only served to harden the resolve of the kibbutz residents. Continually, snipers attempted to kill members of the kibbutz, while others occasionally lobbed mortar shells as close to the houses as possible. Though the British forbade the possession and use of arms by the Jews, the kibbutz insured their survival through regular organized, armed patrols to maintain a safe perimeter. Yankel and Mendel were processed, assigned duties, and integrated into the kibbutz.

One Shabbos afternoon, Yankel and Mendel, who had become best friends, were sitting and talking.

"Do you believe our Promised Land will really become a Jewish state?" Yankel asked.

"Absolutely! The Jewish people won't be denied. We will have our own nation because we've suffered enough and it's the just and fair thing to happen. We will have our own state and we will prosper."

Yankel agreed wholeheartedly. Then, with a smirk, he asked, "Say, Mendel, in case you grow up, what would you like to be?"

Mendel smiled broadly. "I would like to be a tzaddik, a righteous person, and help others who are less fortunate. I have seen the worst of human behavior and I would like to help people rise to their highest level."

Yankel liked this answer. It fit his generous personality. "I applaud you. I'm pleased that you feel that way. Now let's study Hebrew. We have a lot of work to do."

14

FINALITY

APRIL 1947 TO MAY 1948

Mishmar Ha'Emek

On April 4, 1948, the Arab Liberation Army (ALA) commander, Fawzi al-Qawuqji attacked Kibbutz Mishmar Ha'Emek. Both Yankel and Mendel, along with a small force from the kibbutz, had been positioned behind sandbags, waiting for the Arabs to launch their attack. The kibbutz had been conceived and built to occupy a strategic position next to a main road between Jenin and Haifa, a vantage point that allowed the monitoring of all traffic and movement between the two cities. The 150 defenders and two reinforcement companies of Palmach, the fighting arm of the Haganah, added up to a total of slightly less than 300 young fighters. They all waited anxiously for the huge Arab force.

In a softening assault, heavy Arab artillery supplied by the Syrians pounded the kibbutz mercilessly. During the night, the Haganah Golani Brigade filtered into the kibbutz to help repel the ALA attack. The shelling continued the next day, each exploding shell shaking the ground like an earthquake. The attack by the ALA army was relentless; the noise was deafening. On April 7, the British suggested a 24-hour ceasefire, an offer rejected by David Ben-Gurion, the Zionist leader and future Prime Minister of the State of Israel. However, during the 24-hour moratorium—which was welcomed by the Mishmar Ha'Emek defenders—the kibbutz evacuated the women and children.

Yankel and Mendel manned their position in a dugout surrounded by sandbags, with two fighters: Palestinian-born Dudi Frankel and Pincus Goldfarb from Poland. Pincus had been in the Lodz Ghetto and Auschwitz, from which he had luckily managed to escape. Each was fortunate to have a rifle, as there was an acute shortage of weapons and ammunition among the Jews.

"Let them come already!" Pincus shouted.

Dudi tried to calm his three companions. "Be patient. The Arabs take us lightly, but we will have our turn, and we will teach them a lesson."

"Dudi, can you speak Arabic?" Yankel asked.

"Of course. I have many Arab friends who I've grown up with. They're good people, but they tend to get swept up and believe all the propaganda their leaders smother them with."

"I'll stay near you to figure out what they're saying when they start shouting at us," Didi said.

Yankel, Mendel, and the others were finally given orders to advance and clear out surrounding Arab villages to remove any threat to Mishmar Ha'Emek. Though the two friends were exhausted from the ALA shelling and the continual fighting, as were their fellow comrades, they welcomed the idea of moving forward with the kibbutz fighters and giving their attackers some payback. Like an ocean wave, the intensity of the Jewish advance ran over the village of Abu Susha, just north of the kibbutz. The Jewish forces swept forward like a scythe cutting grain, leveling every Arab village in their way. There were some reports that the Jewish forces badly abused the Arabs as they expelled them from their villages, a reaction to the shelling taken earlier, and the loss of friends and loved ones from that shelling. Most of the Arab villagers had fled before the attack reached them, respecting the speed and force of the kibbutz fighters and afraid of their fury.

Yankel, Mendel, and some residents of Mishmar Ha'Emek were ordered to return to the kibbutz to repair the damage done by the heavy artillery.

As they cleared rubble, Mendel said to Yankel, "You know, I'm really glad to be here, in spite of all this fighting. Imagine being a part of establishing a Jewish homeland."

"Yes, I'm glad I'm here too, but I'm also glad my sister is not. Hopefully she and her husband are in America, safe from this chaos."

"I agree. I hope all this turmoil, death, and destruction will have a positive result. Suffering is suffering, whether you're an Arab or a Jew. It's too bad we can't get along and live side by side. After all, we *are all* the children of Abraham—Arabs *and* Jews.

Understanding the Situation

The residents of Kibbutz Mishmar Ha'Emek were physically and mentally exhausted from their battle with the ALA. While there was a great feeling of relief that they had prevailed over such a powerful force, there remained a feeling of tension of what might yet come.

One afternoon, after their victory, Yankel and Mendel sat in a dining hall with a group at lunch and discussed the history behind the present conflict. They were curious to hear and understand what had caused the heightened hostility between Arabs and Jews over the plan for partition. All eyes turned to Dudi, who was the acknowledged scholar of the group.

"Dudi, how did this all come about?" Mendel asked.

"I'll tell you what I know." Dudi cleared his throat. He explained that it started after World War I. The British were given a mandate to govern Palestine, a territory that they had taken from the Turks and their Ottoman Empire in 1937. It was suggested that Palestine be partitioned into two states: a Jewish state and an Arab state, by the Peel Commission, a body established by the British government. This would link the Arab state to Transjordan, and establish a small, independent Jewish state. The British wanted the two sides to agree to the plan, but split opinions among the Jews and outright rejection from the Arabs forced Partition to be shelved. After World War II, the British turned the issue over to the newly formed United Nations. The UN proposed an Arab state and a Jewish state, with Jerusalem as an international entity. The Jewish state was to be 56 percent of

Palestine—which would contain 82 percent of the Jewish population. Even though the idea about Jerusalem being part of the Jewish state was not included in the deal, the Jews accepted the proposal. The majority of Arabs rejected the proposal, confident that they would prevail militarily in the long run. On November 29, 1947, the plan for partition was put to a vote by the United Nations and approved 33 to 13.

"Let me tell you all that while this was going on, the Jews and Arabs were battling each other."

The lunch group sat very quietly, mesmerized by Dudi's clear explanation.

The Jews, looking to the future, were doing everything they could to find weapons, expecting intense armed resistance to the advent of a Jewish homeland. The British did everything they could to keep the Jews from succeeding, consorting many times with the Arabs. The Grand Mufti of Jerusalem, an avowed Nazi supporter during World War II, urged his constituency to destroy the Jews. He painted such a drastic picture of what the Arab fate would be if the Jews prevailed, that large groups of Palestinian Arabs left the country with the hope they could return later, once the dust had settled. Approximately 700,000 Palestinian Arabs left the area in a year's time, with plans to return after the Arabs crushed the Jews. Many others, however, stayed in the land of their birth—willing to live with whatever the outcome of the struggle might be—and would eventually become Israeli citizens.

Thinking Dudi was finished, a few of the lunch group began to clean up their area.

"Just a moment. There's more."

Everyone sat back down, all eyes on Dudi.

"You know, to give birth to a nation is like having a baby. Of course I've never had a baby, but what I mean is that it takes time, and there are pains that come with it."

In America, on May 12, 1948, US President Harry Truman met with General George C. Marshal, Secretary of State; Clark Clifford, Presidential Advisor; and other advisors to discuss whether or not the US should support the proposal for a State of Israel. General

Marshall and the State Department were against supporting a new Jewish state, mainly because it would affect America's ability to get Arab oil. Clark Clifford, however, voted for support of a new Jewish state.

"While this debate was going on, our wonderful spokesman, Abba Eban—who, by the way, spoke ten languages—continually pleaded the Jewish case to the United Nations and the world. To anyone who'd listen."

"Then what? What happened?" someone shouted.

"A minute please."

"So?"

"Harry Truman, representing the United States, was the first to vote in favor of a Jewish homeland."

Someone exclaimed loudly, "God bless Harry Truman. He's a tzaddik, a righteous person!"

Dudi smiled.

"Joseph Stalin, representing Russia, was the second to vote. Unbelievably, he also voted in favor of the State of Israel."

A rumble of commentary ran through the group of rapt listeners.

"Our fellow Jews around the world were glued to their radios, giving their heartfelt support. You can imagine the excitement felt by Jews around the world when, on May 14, 1948, Israel was declared a state by the United Nations. Unimaginable! A dedicated Jewish homeland, where all Jews were welcome. On the other hand, as soon as David Ben-Gurion announced the birth of the State of Israel, the Arabs attacked. And here we are. As you all know, we were attacked prior to the State of Israel officially becoming legitimate, and we will be at it again, I'm sure. That's it. We are not just wandering Jews anymore. We are Israeli Jews."

A big round of applause thundered for Dudi, with a sea of smiles that lit up the room.

Canada

In Winnipeg, Canada, Lena looked at Schmuel, who seemed lost in a dream or a thought. "Why are you so distant these last few days?" she asked.

He looked up, his mind coming back to the surface. "I sometimes forget who I am. Now I've got a new name: Samuel or Sam, as they call me here in Canada. I feel useless being here while my fellow Jews are fighting to survive yet again, this time in our Promised Land. I'm not used to sitting around while others do the fighting. Remember when we watched the UN vote in the newsreels and clapped our hands and shouted when Jewish Palestine became a home to the Jews, when it became the State of Israel. Now, any Jew can go there and be among his own kind. No antisemitism, no pogroms. It's our sanctuary, where we have the opportunity to achieve and live our lives without limits. But that sanctuary is surrounded by hostile Arabs who say they will drive the Jews into the sea. I even heard that an Egyptian general claimed that fighting the Jews would be 'a parade without any risks' and that the Arabs will be in Tel Aviv in two weeks. There are thousands in their armies who are well-trained and who are filled with hatred for the Jews. They are carrying modern weapons while the Jews are short of everything: vehicles, armor, cannons, guns, and ammunition. The Jews have no air force, no navy, and no tanks. Most of the people who fight for Israel have not had any training or experience in making war. They are the remnants of the death camps and displaced persons. Lena, I am here, and they are there. I enjoy a peaceful, fulfilling life while they continue to wonder if they'll be alive tomorrow or the week after. This is so frustrating."

"Darling, listen to me," Lena said softly, with loving concern in her voice. "The Jews will prevail, just as I know that someday I will be reunited with my brother. The fighting between the Arabs and the Jews in Palestine has been going on for decades, even with the British there. The Jews voted for partition and now have their own homeland. The Arabs in Palestine didn't vote for partition and now they have nothing. The other Arab countries, with their big armies, really don't care about the Palestinians. I heard that the Syrians want a piece of northern Israel, and the Egyptians want whatever they can get in Sinai, Gaza, and in the south of the new land. King Abdullah, the ruler of Transjordan who has shown some signs of consideration for the Jews, would like to have Jerusalem for his own kingdom. The Iraqis want whatever they can get. Actually, Lebanon, with its large Christian population, wasn't too enthusiastic about participating in the war. They're a house divided to start with!"

"How do you know so much about this?"

"I have ears and eyes, a brain, and opinions," Lena said, proud of her answer. "Jewish communities around the world are concerned about everything that is happening with our people. I heard of volunteers making arrangements to go to Israel and fight. Others are working hard to get money for weapons. You know Schmuel, Sol, and Anna are there, and I know no one's going to mess with our partisan friends. Besides, God owes us a favor."

"I hope so, Lena. I really hope so."

Mandate Ends

On May 14, 1948, the British Mandate ended and David Ben-Gurion (Israel's first prime minister), in an historic announcement to the world, proclaimed the new Jewish State of Israel—a home and hope for all Jewish people. The Arab armies of Egypt, Syria, Iraq, Lebanon, and Transjordan—with help from Saudi Arabia—pounced on the new State of Israel. These armies were all well-trained and equipped with huge quantities of weapons. Since there were no longer British naval blockades, weapons and people started flowing into Israel. Of course, the war between the Arabs and the Jews had actually started long before, right under the watchful eyes of the British, but now the battle would go on until the last one standing.

The original partition proposed by the UN would leave Israel with indefensible borders, but since the Arabs voted against that plan, all options were open. Yankel and Mendel, along with all the new immigrants to Israeli, were on constant alert. There were recent arrivals of Jews, even gentiles, everywhere as the nation defended itself against the Arab onslaught. A new commander, Zechial Rotkin, came to Mishmar Ha-Edek, to gather soldiers to defend the Galilee. Rotkin was a congenial fellow and very knowledgeable. He had been part of the Jewish Brigade Group in Italy and was well-trained. He met with the kibbutz defenders to explain his objectives. Yankel and Mendel appreciated the opportunity to learn more about the conflict.

Yankel asked the commander where all the weapons were coming from.

Rotkin explained that in 1946, Ben-Gurion saw the need to acquire weapons so the new state-to-be could arm itself against the Arabs when the time came. He put a mass covert arms acquisition campaign into motion. "Czechoslovakia has been a big help, a blessing, in selling us arms and military equipment, among other suppliers." The Czechs have not only supplied weapons but sold Israel 25 Avia S-199 airplanes. They are a poor version of the ME 109 Messerschmitt and are also called 'mules,' but we're happy to have them." Rotkin continued. "Agents in the US purchased three secondhand B-17 bombers, which were used to bomb Cairo in July. It was an unhappy surprise for the Egyptians. The new state had been buying whatever weapons it could get, including half-tracks, tanks, and light machine guns.

"Who paid for all this? Where did all the money come from?"

"From our fellow Jews in America and England, South Africa, Canada, Australia, and around the world who worked every day to make money available. But let me tell you the best part: while all this was going on, we were making our own bullets right here in Israel, right under the nose of the British, in a place called the Ayalon Institute. We even used their electricity. Can you imagine? The Jews built an underground factory that was disguised by a laundry at one end and a bakery on the other end. They actually produced 40,000 bullets a day, and this with only 45 people."

A rumble of soft-spoken voices filled the room as the kibbutz defenders leaned over to one another, commenting on the incredible story.

Rotkin held up his hand for silence. At that point, someone waved at the commander, to let him know that he had to leave for another meeting but would see us at dinner.

Mendel, who had been fascinated by the commander's explanation, happily soaking it up, leaned closer to Yankel and said in a hushed voice, "A guy told me we not only have airplanes and tanks, but we also have a navy."

"You're kidding! Where did we get a navy?"

"Listen, we have three ships. One is a US Coast Guard Cutter, and we have two British icebreakers."

"That's a navy?" Yankel asked.

"I'm not done. They're outfitted with canons on deck and they successfully bombed the Egyptians off of Gaza. I'll tell you, we have so much to be proud of, and yet there's so much still left to do."

"There sure is."

Suddenly, Mendel's face changed expression as if he'd forgotten something important. "Yankel, in all the time I've known you, I've never asked you if you have any family that survived the Nazis and their death camps."

"I have been blessed to have a sister who survived. Besides her, I really don't know."

"Where is she?"

"I'm not sure, but I do know she is married to a friend of mine who was in Dachau with me"

"No kidding! I was in Dachau for a while. What was your friend's name?"

"His name was Avrum."

"Avrum. Hmm, I knew a guy named Avrum. He was a young guy, a tailor."

"Now you are kidding!" Yankel said with delight. My Avrum was a tailor. I think maybe it's the same guy. He was a real mensch."

"Where are they?"

"Well, Avrum wanted to go to America, so I hope that's what happened."

"What a small world!" Mendel replied. "By the way, I met a girl yesterday. Her name is Shoshona and she is a flower of beauty. You should find a girl too."

"I will. We will make many little Israelis. They will grow and prosper in our newfound home. This is a unique country. It's made up of a people who have been singled out to be killed. In the camps there was no unity, no support. But we are finished with dying alone, dying for nothing. We're one people, dedicated to living together and, if necessary, dying together. We've lived through death camps, so who better than us to understand the value of life."

Mohamed Ali Hadad

The crisp, bitter cold of the desert night made Mohamed Ali Hadad shiver. He and his friend, Ebrahim Awad Bitar, were getting ready to attack a Jewish kibbutz in southern Palestine. The two friends were part of an Egyptian military force moving up from the Sinai with the goal to reach Tel Aviv. So far, they had encountered virtually no opposition. Their next assignment was to capture the Jewish settlement, Yad Mordechai. They enjoyed a few minutes of rest while waiting for half-tracks and tanks to maneuver into place.

"What are we doing?" Mohamed asked Ebrahim. "What is the purpose of being here instead of at home with our families?"

"We have to drive the Jews into the sea."

"Why? What difference does it make to us?"

"The Jews don't belong in Palestine. Palestine belongs to our brothers, the Palestinians."

"According to who?" Ebrahim challenged.

"According to our officers."

Just then, their good friend Hassan Said Awad appeared. "Hey, what's going on here? You both look so serious."

"We're discussing the land of Palestine," Mohamed answered. "The question we're discussing is who does Palestine really belong to: Palestinian Arabs or the Jews? The Palestinians say it's theirs and the Jews say it belongs to them."

Hassan thought for a moment. His two friends stared at him intently, waiting for an answer. He looked at his two friends coyly. "I'm glad you brought that up. Yesterday I talked with Lieutenant Nazri, who was a teacher at Cairo University. I took a class taught by him a few years back. He told me that the Jews make up 82 percent of the population in Palestine. He says that one of the reasons we need to take over this land is so that it ends up being under Arab control."

"That really doesn't answer the question," Ebrahim said. "I mean, who was here first? That was a long time ago. Nobody really knows who came first?"

"I have also heard that the Jews claim that their God promised them this land."

"What does our God say?"

"When their God made that promise were there any people living here already?"

Mohamed raised his hand to speak. "This is crazy, you know. I don't see what's here that's worth fighting for. It's a small land with nothing special about it. The British have been running it, but the Jews have made the majority of improvements. The city of Jerusalem is sacred to both the Arabs and the Jews. Why not share?"

"Neither side will compromise," Hassan said. "So here we are: Egyptians, moving to capture the same piece of land coveted by the Syrians, the Lebanese, the Iraqis, and the Jordanians. None of us seem to care who it really belongs to, as long as we get a piece of it. It's crazy. Just think, the Jews are the children of our Father, who we call Ibrahem, and they call Abraham. Praise to Allah, I hope He will sort it out."

"Have either of you ever meet a Jew?" Ebrahim asked.

"Yes," Mohamed said, "I bought a kettle from a Jewish merchant in Cairo just last year."

"Did he cheat you?"

"No. In fact, we drank tea together after the purchase. My father knew his father. It's sad to think we are here fighting someone else's battle against people we don't even know and who have done nothing bad to us—in spite of our officers assuring us that this will be an easy battle, if there's even a battle at all."

Ebrahim stared blankly off into the distance and muttered quietly, "Not to those who will die."

"Yes," Mohamed sighed, "not to those."

Yad Mordechai

Sol and Anna were ecstatic about ending up at Yad Mordechai. It was in the south, close to the Mediterranean Sea and, best of all, it was warm. Both of them were gladly accepted into the kibbutz family. The fact that they had been partisans gave them a certain prestige. It was no secret that when the British Mandate ended, the Arabs would attempt to level the kibbutz, but all of Yad Mordechai's members were invested in its survival and had prepared—as best they could—for whatever was to happen. The kibbutz had been built on a hill and dominated the coastal road just above Gaza. Everyone at Yad Mordechai had their duties. Sol was happy to be teaching children again, as well as work with the military.

While Yad Mordechai felt like heaven to both of them, to Sol it was more than that. It was a tonic for him that he could once again be a teacher. He liked looking into the eyes of his students and seeing the wonder in their faces as they received information on history, science, math, and other concepts new to them. He decided that Jews were a curious people who wanted to know anything and everything they could about the world around them and how it affected them. They were bred to learn. One of the best parts of teaching again was that he really liked the head of the school system on the kibbutz: Simeon Lipshitz. Simmy, as he was called, was a tall, regal-looking man with an easy smile for everyone. He was also from Poland, so there was a natural bond between them.

One day, the two teachers were talking about a variety of things and Sol asked Simmy what his favorite subject was.

"History. I love it. Here we are in a land that is rich with history. If you dig down even a little bit, you're likely to find an old civilization waiting for you. And if you keep digging, I'll bet you'll find another, older civilization. Since this is our Promised Land, I believe we need to promise to keep and preserve it not only for the generations of Jews to come, but also for the rest of the world, because their roots can be found somewhere here too. The archaeologists can have a field day here. You know, history reminds us of who we are. In so many ways, we are like the people who came before us."

Sol became fascinated listening to Simmy. He had missed these intellectual discussions. They were stimulating and uplifting.

"You know, Sol, sometimes I think the Jews are like the Ballad of Sir Andrew."

"Sir Andrew? Who was that?"

Simmy softly chuckled. "I'm not sure I know and I'm not sure I remember exactly the correct quotation, but let me tell you the quote as I remember it:

"Fight on my men, Sir Andrew says,
I'm just now wounded, but not yet slain.
I'll just lie down and rest awhile,
And then I'll rise up and fight again."

Sol gave a long sigh with a soft little whistle of appreciation. This ode was so powerful.

"That's what the Jews are doing, Sol. We have been wounded, but now is our time to rise up and fight again!"

"Amen, Simmy. Amen!"

One day Anna came up to Sol, with something obviously on her mind. "Sol, I have something to tell you that you don't know about."

"Really?" Sol said in a sarcastic tone. "What could it be that you know, and I don't?"

"Don't you want to guess?"

"Oy, vey! What are you making such a fuss about?"

Anna smiled and glanced down at her tummy. Her eyes sparkled with mischief.

Sol stood like a frozen pillar of ice, his eyes widened in realization.

"Sol, say something. Don't just stare."

"Oh my God, Anna, what a blessing! You... I mean, we are going to have a child? Vey es mir! Think of it, life goes on, and we are a part of the process. You know, it's early May 1948, and the British Mandate will end in a few days. Things could get crazy here. What will we do? How can we protect our child?"

"We'll do whatever we must, my love, and we will be protected by the hand of God.

I feel it and I know it. Mazel tov to us. Our family of two will become three."

South of Yad Mordechai, Major General Ahmad Ali al-Mwawi had divided his large force of Egyptians into two units: one to proceed to Jerusalem, the other to Tel Aviv. On their way to Tel Aviv, the soldiers had bypassed many small settlements without engaging any of them. But Yad Mordechai was too big to ignore, and it sat directly in the way of their destination. The Egyptian army numbered 2,500 soldiers to the kibbutz's paltry 130 defenders. Plus, they had air support, heavy armor, and artillery.

The kibbutz leaders explained the situation to their people without trying to soften it. While news of the overwhelming Egyptian force was terrifying, it had really been expected by the kibbutz defenders. They knew that some would die, but the leaders unfolded a plan that included survival.

"We can and must delay them, hopefully with the help of some Palmachniks (young fighters from the Haganah), but in the end we will retreat. We'll lower the loss of life, by being willing to lose the kibbutz. If we can delay them, it will give our new homeland the time it needs to bring in more weapons and more fighters."

The kibbutz members decided to immediately evacuate all the children and some of the women. On May 18, a small Israeli armored column arrived and took away a small group of women and 92 children. This left the kibbutz with 110 defenders, 20 of which were women, plus two squads of the Palmach, who were equipped only with light weapons, a medium machine gun, and a hand-held anti-tank weapon.

On May 19, the Egyptian artillery started pounding the settlement. The defenders hunkered down in their sandbagged defensive positions, awaiting the main attack, which began in the afternoon. The Egyptians attacked with two battalions of infantry and one armored battalion.

"Holy shit!" Sol shouted to his friend Yossi upon seeing the Egyptians heading toward them. "How many are there?"

"Enough for us all."

The din of firing weapons tested the defenders' ears. In the beginning, the Egyptians breached the perimeter fence, but the dug-in defenders exacted a heavy toll on the invaders. After 3 hours of intense fighting, the Egyptians retreated, leaving dozens of their dead behind. The kibbutz toll was 5 dead and 11 wounded. The next day, the Egyptians attacked repeatedly, and were be repulsed every time. Thirteen Israelis died and 20 were wounded. The Egyptians suffered heavy losses in the attacks.

That night the Palmach managed to send in a platoon of reinforcements, including six British deserters with a few more weapons. Sol was worried about Anna. In the heavy fighting, there was no opportunity to change positions or locations without being exposed to heavy fire. In between assaults, the Egyptian artillery and tanks, as well as their air force, pounded the kibbutz, leveling buildings and rearranging the landscape.

On May 23, the Arab infantry, with armored support, advanced into the kibbutz. The night before, the defenders, exhausted from fighting and low on ammunition, got permission to withdraw, which they did quietly. The Egyptians did not realize the defenders were gone and shelled the compound for four more hours before advancing and taking over what was left of Yad Mordechai.

Surrounded by the chaos of battle, Sol managed to find Anna—a virtual miracle. They shared a precious moment when they realized they were both alive.

"Anna, my love, these last few days have been a nightmare, but the three of us are still here: me, you, and our baby. But I think that while all of us are sad for our fallen brothers and sisters, we're proud that such a small force could hold up a whole army. The delay will be costly to them, both in time and morale. I'm so proud to be here among my fellow Jews."

15

NEW WORLD, NEW LIFE
MAY 1962 TO JUNE 1967

Cleveland, 1962

Avrum had just eaten a wonderful dinner with his family, prepared by Mollie. At the dinner table he enjoyed the chatter of his sons and their playful prodding of one another. He sat at the table after his kids had gone out to play and watched Mollie at the sink as she cleaned the dishes and pots. "Mollie dear, can you believe we are here in America? Can you believe that we just had a dinner with our children, a dinner that we would have never believed could happen when we were still in Poland. Imagine, my love, here we are, survivors they call us, as Americans living a Jewish life without duress or fear. Can you believe we have lived to see a Jewish homeland? And in two months our son Joshua will have his Bar Mitzvah."

"We're blessed, my love. I could never have dreamed of a life like this."

"God, how I wish our parents and families could have been here to see and enjoy these moments."

"Yes," Mollie sighed. "If only."

"At least your brother is coming, all the way from Israel, and bringing his family, just to be at the Bar Mitzvah. I can't find the words to express my feelings about that. It will be so great to see Yankel again. How I wish Lena could also be here to share this special time, but we should be thankful and, as they say here, 'count our blessings.'"

Mollie dropped the wet dishtowel on the sink, took off her apron, and came to the table, where she took a seat next to Avrum. She took both his hands in hers and looked deeply into his moist eyes "Avi, you're right, we are so lucky. We are living our lives for those who have passed away. I feel good every day that we are living as Jews. We are teaching our children the responsibilities and philosophies they should know about being Jewish."

Avrum squeezed her hands tightly and quietly nodded.

"Okay then," Mollie smiled. "No more time to talk, my love. You keep working with Josh so he gets everything right at his Bar Mitzvah and I have to start baking!"

Events in Cleveland

Moving to Cleveland from New Orleans was a good decision for Avrum, Mollie, and their children. Cleveland was much more like the areas in Poland that they were used to. They liked the people and especially enjoyed being close to Mollie's family. Even before all the boxes were unpacked, they joined Park Synagogue, a Conservative temple.

The year was going to be special because their oldest son was going to beBar Mitzvahed—an unforgettable event for all of them. Josh had studied hard for three years and now the golden moment was fast approaching when he would officially become a man, according to the rites of Bar Mitsvah. Avrum always had to laugh when he took Josh to his weekly Hebrew lessons, because he wore either his Little League uniform or his basketball shorts. As they say, "only in America."

Josh had a good friend, Tyler Berman, who was to have his Bar Mitzvah two months before Josh. Tyler's parents were good friends of Avrum and Mollie and their families socialized a lot. He and his family belonged to Beth Israel, a Reformed synagogue. Avrum was interested to see how different Tyler's Bar Mitzvah was going to be compared to Josh's.

The Bielinski family arrived at Tyler's Bar Mitzvah a bit earlier than most to get good seats. Josh sat with his friends while Avrum and Mollie and their other children sat together. The Bar Mitzvah went quite well. Avrum watched Tyler's father, Jay, glow with pride as he sat up on the bima, the stage where Tyler performed in front of the whole congregation. It was a long ceremony, although a little shorter than Josh's would be when his time came. The Reform Bar Mitzvah ceremony was usually, but not always, the shortest, with the Conservative ceremony a bit longer, and the Orthodox the longest.

After the Bar Mitzvah, everybody was invited to a lunch downstairs in the synagogue. Avrum's kids couldn't wait, especially because there was a fabulous table of assorted baked desserts. Avrum and Mollie congratulated Jay and his wife, Mary, and went through the buffet line for a delicious lunch. While Avrum was hungry to begin with, he became even hungrier from the fragrance of the food. He took his plate, loaded with traditional delicacies, to an open table and sat down to eat.

"Is anyone sitting here?" a voice asked.

Avrum looked up to see a young Catholic priest pointing at the chair next to him. "No, it's yours. You're welcome to sit and enjoy."

As the priest settled into the chair, he told Avrum his name was Father McCarthy.

"Nice to meet you, Father. I'm Avrum Bielinski. Did you enjoy the ceremony?"

"Very much. Are all Bar Mitzvahs like this one?"

"Similar, but the ones at the Conservative synagogues, and especially the Orthodox ones, are more intense. I belong to Park Synagogue, a Conservative temple."

"Ah, yes, this is my first Bar Mistvah. It's fascinating."

"Say, my son is having his Bar Mitzvah in two months. If you're interested, I'd like to invite you to come and see how we conservative Jews do it. Give me your information and I'll send you an invitation."

"How nice of you. Yes, I'd love to come to your ceremony." The priest gave Avrum his contact information, accompanied by a warm smile. "May I ask where you are from?"

"Originally from Poland, Father, but now I am an American, thanks to God."

"Were you part of the Holocaust?"

"Yes," Avrum said. "But now I'm in America enjoying the freedom... and the food. Please, I'd like you to join me for lunch."

Josh's Bar Mitzvah

The great day of Josh's Bar Mitzvah was finally here. Avrum and Mollie, with input from Josh, and a great deal of head scratching, had purchased a beautiful tallis, the prayer shawl he would use for the rest of his life. Arrangements had been made for a lunch after the Bar Mitzvah was finished. Mollie and her friends had baked for days and the aroma in the Bielinski house was a delight. Invitations had gone out to friends and family and Avrum and Mollie were ecstatic that Yankel and his family were coming. Mollie could hardly sit still waiting to see her brother again. Josh invited all his friends, including his Little League team, and Avrum invited Father McCarthy, as well as many others.

The arrival of Yankel and his family couldn't have been a more joyous event. The two families cried and laughed and smothered one another with love and happiness. Mollie and Yankel couldn't stop touching and hugging each other. Avrum embraced Yankel and whispered into his ear, "Come, let us have a moment together."

The two friends disappeared into Avrum's study.

"So Yankel, you're looking well. And what a family you have! I couldn't have wished for anything more for you. God knows the pain and suffering we went through, and now here we are, some of the precious few who have seen the worst of it and survived."

Yankel nodded in agreement and sighed. "So true."

"What's it like to be in Israel, such a small nation in the middle of a sea of hostile Arabs?"

"It's wonderful," Yankel glowed. "I'm surrounded by Jews, and to tell you the truth, I don't feel as though I'm in danger. I know that you and Mollie and your family are in a good place, as well. The support of the Jewish people in the United States is a comfort and blessing for Israel. Is America everything you thought it would be?"

"Oh, yes. Even more. America is a very special place. It's a mix of people from all over the world who live together and blend into one nation. And as you said, it's one of the most important supporters of Israel."

"Thank goodness."

"It's a pleasure to watch my children grow up with the opportunity to be what they want to be, but you know, we—you and I—and the other Holocaust survivors need to tell our story to as many people as we can. They need to know the truth."

"A very good point. We can never allow this piece of history to disappear. It took courage—and a lot of luck—to live through it."

"Absolutely!" Avrum smiled. "And look where we are now."

"Yes," Yankel said, returning Avrum's smile.

"Well, my good friend, here we are, preaching to one another. Let's have a schnapps and rejoin our families. We have so much to celebrate."

On the Friday night before the Bar Mitsvah, Avrum and Mollie presented Josh with his very own tallis during services at the synagogue. It was all Avrum could do to keep his hands steady as he straightened out the prayer shawl on his son's shoulders. Mollie glowed with love and pride. Avrum was close to tears just thinking about being in a new country, living a new life, and passing on ancient Jewish traditions that would live beyond his own time in future generations.

Saturday arrived and the Bielinskis went to the synagogue early to prepare for the full Bar Mitzvah ceremony. Yankel and his family met them on the temple stairs, brimming with excitement. After exchanging hugs and kisses, they entered the temple, where Yankel found good seats and Avrum walked to the bima with Josh. As Avrum sat in a plush chair on the bima, he looked at his son standing before the dais and choked up. He was so proud of him. What a moment to remember!

The synagogue filled up with friends, family, and congregants as the service moved forward. The Torahs were removed from the ark and family members and friends were called up to participate in the ceremony. Meanwhile, Avrum was lost in his own thoughts. *Momma, Poppa; my grandparents, Bobba, and Zeda; and Uncle Nathan too, I can feel you. You are here with us sharing this moment. And my dear sister, Lena, I feel that you are also here. I know you are safe and well. This moment is for you too. I am sure I will see you again.* He was awakened from of his thoughts as he was called up to say a prayer with Mollie. He glanced out at the audience. Everyone was paying full attention, taking in the ceremony.

Then Josh stepped up to read from the Torah. He had studied for this moment for more than three years. He flawlessly chanted the ancient Hebrew words before him. His voice was clear and smooth as he intoned the ancient prayers with meaning and confidence. Finally, the ceremony ended, and everyone went to the lunch buffet, which was beautifully laid out.

Family and friends came up to Avrum and Mollie with congratulations and enthusiastic comments on the ceremony. Father McCarthy was among the well-wishers. He had a big smile on his face as he told Avrum how much he enjoyed the whole ceremony, especially the camaraderie of all the participants and those who attended. He said he would be giving him a call and, after shaking hands, the priest left. Avrum went about the pleasure of mingling with his guests and sharing the delights of the event.

Teaching Class

The advent of Josh's Bar Mitzvah had brought back nostalgic memories of the past. Avrum and Mollie had performed their duty as good Jewish parents as they helped and supported their son through the process. Avrum was sad it was over, but he had other children who would also have their turn.

The phone rang.

"Hello, Avrum here."

"Mr. Bielinski, this is Father McCarthy."

"Father McCarthy! How nice to hear from you. To what do I owe the pleasure?"

"First, I want to take the opportunity to thank you for your kindness for inviting me to your son's Bar Mitzvah. I felt like I was witnessing a moment in history as I watched your son perform the continuing tradition of your people. I realized what dedication and preparation had gone into the event. It was beautiful."

"Thank you very much, Father."

"The reason I called was to ask if you would be willing to come to our school, St. Ignatius High School, and tell us about what it's like to be Jewish."

"Well, I'm not sure if I'm qualified to do that. There might be many questions that I can't answer."

"Oh, no, not at all. The class will be low key, and Father John and I will be present to help, if needed. Perhaps you could speak a little about the Holocaust and your transition to American life. It would be invaluable for our boys to hear your story."

"Okay, I'll give it a try. Give me a time and place and I'll be there."

"Great! Would Tuesday 24 be okay, 10 a.m. at St. Ignatius High School? The class will be an hour long."

"I'll be there, Father. See you then."

Avrum hung up the phone and immediately asked himself, *What have you gotten yourself into?* He decided he would go to the library and study up on some Jewish history and traditions, not knowing what he would be asked.

The day for the class arrived too soon for comfort. Here he was, his mind in a whirl. He thought, *Here I go. Another life adventure.* Mollie had been encouraging him to do something like this, and he had thought about doing it if he escaped the war alive. When he arrived at the school, he was relieved to find Father McCarthy waiting for him at the door. The priest explained that he had consolidated two classes into one and there would be about 50 students involved. Avrum had made a few notes and was as ready as he could be. He had decided that in the short time he had, he would speak for approximately 20 minutes and then answer questions during the remaining time. The students entered and took their seats. Then, the school bell rang.

Avrum introduced himself and started by telling the class about his life in Poland. Then, he talked about his time at the concentration camp in Dachau. He followed that with his journey to America, and he told them how he got to Cleveland. Lastly, he explained how he had met Father McCarthy. The rapt looks on their faces gave him confidence to speak more freely. He could see the class was fascinated by his experiences in Dachau. Finally, the time came for questions.

"Are you mad at the Germans for what they did?" a student asked.

"I hold nothing against today's Germans. However, personally, I cannot forgive Hitler and his henchmen for the destruction of whole families and the cruelty they displayed."

The questions continued and he answered them one by one.

A student raised his hand and stood up. "I have a friend who says the Holocaust never happened." The boy sat down, leaving the statement hanging.

Avrum took a breath to collect himself. Denial of the Holocaust infuriated him. He answered in slow, carefully measured words, afraid that he'd lose it. "Young man, your friend is badly misinformed. Just a moment." With that statement, Avrum took off his jacket and rolled up his sleeve, exposing the tattoo on his arm given to him by the Nazis at Dachau.

All the boys leaned forward to see it.

"This tattoo reminds me every day of my life that there was a Holocaust and that we should always remember what happened and never let it happen again." He rolled down his sleeve and looked at his watch. "Time for maybe two more questions."

Another hand went up. "Mr. Bielinski, do you have nightmares about your life in the concentration camp?"

"Every day of my life, I remember what happened to me and how lucky I am to have survived, especially when so many have died. A day never passes that I don't ask myself why I survived when others did not. I continually think of my lost family and especially of my little sister, Lena, who I've tried to find but have not been able to so far. I thank God for the family I have and the good fortune to have ended up in such a wonderful country as America. Yes, there are difficult moments, but I am here, and I always count my blessings."

He looked at the students as they stared at him, hanging on every word of his comments.

One boy who was noticeably attentive kept raising his hand and Avrum finally called on him.

"Yes, you there," Avrum pointed.

"You've said that even though you have searched for your sister and haven't been able to locate her, that you feel she is somewhere safe, and you think you will find her. What makes you think that will ever happen?"

Avrum often wrestled with that question himself. "Well, my father brought her to a trusted Polish couple to hide and protect her. That couple, in order to further protect her, put her in a Catholic convent, where the sisters kept her safe. Finally, she and two friends left the convent and found a group of Jewish partisans who were fighting the Germans. The leader of the partisans was the older brother of one of Lena's friends from the convent. That is where I lost track of her. It's been frustrating beyond reason to not be able to find her, but I just know she was safe and made it through the war. There's hope, always hope and faith. Every day I walk the streets looking at faces, hoping one of them will be hers."

He then scanned the eager faces of the class. "And now, one last question."

A tall, good-looking boy jumped up. "Mr. Bielinski, why do the Jews have all the money?"

Avrum hesitated in disbelief at the question, not knowing exactly how to answer. Then he turned to Father McCarthy. "Father, isn't the Catholic church the richest religious institution in the world?"

The nodding heads and murmurs surprised Avrum. They understood!

"Yes," the priest replied. "Now let us all thank Mr. Bielinski for his time and the wonderful presentation he gave us."

Loud applause erupted, drowning out Avrum's sigh of relief.

Our Son, Solly

Canada was everything that Schmuel and Lena hoped it would be. They were citizens in a country where every person was regarded as an equal. Originally a nation of refugees, Canada honored the right of all to do their best to determine their own futures. Jews, Christians, and Muslims alike, lived side by side in peace.

Schmuel's and Meir's trucking business had grown at a healthy rate. It provided a good living for both families. Canada had been the sanctuary they had dreamed of and a wonderful place to raise their children. Two of Schmuel and Lena's children went to Kent State University. After graduation they both got good jobs in the area. The other two children also went to college in the USA and located locally, as well.

One day Schmuel and Meir met to discuss their business. Schmuel started the conversation. "Meir, we have done quite well in our trucking business, and I was thinking it would be a healthy thing if we opened a branch in the USA. Lena and I have our children living there and we could be close to them. We could see our grandchildren on a regular basis and perhaps in time our children could come into the business. What do you think?

"Well, Schmuel, if you can believe, I was thinking along the same lines. I think it's a good idea. The best part is that you don't have to learn a new language."

The brothers had a good laugh together and hugged.

Ten days earlier, Schmuel had sat with his family in Congregation Shaarey Zedek, Winnipeg's oldest synagogue, celebrating the Jewish new year, Rosh Hashanah. He and Lena both prayed that she would one day soon be reunited with her brother. They were surrounded by fellow Jews as they listened to the sounding of the shofar, the ancient ram's horn that is played during services to remind us that we area a continuation of Jewish history.

"Tekiah!" the rabbi chanted, to usher in the sound of hope for the future.

The clear, triumphant notes of the shofar rang out, surrounding everyone in the service like a protective cloak. Schmuel peeked at his family. Lena stood with their sons and daughter. Next to them stood Schmuel's brother, Meir, with his family. Who could have envisioned this day? How proud their parents would have been.

A few days later, Schmuel's oldest son, Solly, came to him and told him he had just heard that Israel was being attacked by Egypt, Syria, and other Arab states. Egypt had entered the Sinai Peninsula in the south of Israel and Syria was attacking Israel from the Golan Heights in the north. Both of these territories were captured by Israel in a previous war with the Arabs and had been kept as a political necessity by Israel so it could protect itself. Solly—named after Schmuel's good friend, Sol, from his partisan days—was infuriated that Israel should be attacked on the holiest Jewish day of the year.

"Pop," he said, "I want to go there and fight. I already talked to my good friend, Jerry Baskin and he wants to go too."

"Whoa, just a moment, Solly. The Israelis can take care of themselves, I'm sure. There is no need for you go there and get yourself shot."

"But there *is* a need. We have to stand together and support each other. What kind of a Jew would I be if I did not join and help my fellow Jews?"

Schmuel's memories of his own youth, when he was the same age as his son, flooded his mind. He had no immediate answer. He lovingly put his hand on Solly's shoulder. "Let me think about it. I have to talk with your mother," he said softly.

Solly glared at him for a moment. Then his scowl turned into a smile, and they hugged.

"Okay Pop, let's talk tomorrow. But remember, I really want to go."

Schmuel thought to himself, *Your son is just like you.*

16

AVRUM AND JACOB
MAY 2002

At the Park

"Grandpa, this is a new friend of mine. I met her last week at Sunday school. Her name is Sophie. Sophie, this is my Grandpa Avrum."

"I'm pleased to meet you," Sophie said politely.

"Hello, Sophie." Avrum smiled as he studied her face. "That's such a nice name. It was my mother's name."

"Grandpa Avrum was just telling me a few things from a long time ago." He paused. "Grandpa, is it okay for Sophie to hear?"

Avrum nodded. His smile softened with concern. "Sure Jacob, but you know, there are so many bad memories that I would rather not talk about."

"I already know something about it. We study World War II in school and Sunday School, too."

Sophie stood, transfixed, studying the interchange between grandfather and grandson. She seemed mesmerized by the deep respect and love between them.

"Grandpa," Jacob said, "I always hear you humming a song. What is it?"

"Oh, I don't even realize I do that. It's a song from long ago. My mother used to sing it to my sister and me at bedtime."

"Does it have words?"

"Well, yes, it does."

"Will you sing it for Sophie and me?"

"Oh yes, I would like that," Sophie chimed in enthusiastically.

Avrum's smile became a mixture of surprise and thoughtful decision. The full smile returned, with a little sparkle in his eyes. "Okay. It's been a long time, but I'll give it a try."

He straightened up, and quietly cleared his throat. His eyes looked upward and away, as if trying to recapture a long-lost memory. He began.

> "Little child, little child, go to sleep.
> Whatever you dream is yours to keep.
> So close your eyes and—"

Sophie interrupted with excitement. "I know that song!"

"How could you possibly know that song?"

"My grandma has sung that song to me many times, she..." Sophie stopped and turned her head to a figure walking toward them.

"Oh, look! Here she comes now. That's my Grandma Lena."

EPILOGUE

Every year in the village of Leszno, Poland, the Catholic convent receives an anonymous donation. In the beginning, it came from Canada, but more recently it has come from the United States.

In a forest in Israel, where trees are planted to honor righteous people, there are two trees side by side: one is for Mother Zofia, the other for her husband Farmer Jan, their kindness and bravery not forgotten.

Yankel Abramowicz, Avrum's good friend and Mollie's brother, reached Palestine where he fought in Israel's War of Independence. He was later wounded in the Six-Day War and still walks with a limp. He married a sabra—an Israeli girl—and they have five children. The children regularly visit their cousins, who now live in Cleveland, Ohio.

Mendel and Shoshana married after the War of Independence. Shoshona gave Mendel four wonderful daughters. Two became doctors and two became teachers. Mendel's family and Yankel's family remain close.

Sol and Anna made it to Palestine with the help of the Jewish Brigade Group soldiers and also fought in the War of Independence. Sol returned to being a teacher, his original occupation in Poland. Sol and Anna live in Petah Tikvah with their three children and six grandchildren.

Meir found the love of his life, or perhaps we should say she found him. He and his brother Schmuel became partners in the trucking business. Meir and his family currently live in Manitoba, Canada. He is a big participant in the activities of his local synagogue. One of his children has made aliyah—immigration to Israel—and lives close to Sol and Anna.

Colonel Helmut Dietrick accepted his orders and led his men against the Russian army in Estonia at the Battle of Narva. He survived, but lost control over his left arm. After the war, he returned to his wife, Marta, and his two children. He worked hard to build a life in a beaten and battered Germany. He and his family lived in Frankfurt where he taught Political Science at Goethe University, a relatively liberal school, until his retirement. He actively lobbied for minority rights.

Lena and Schmuel moved from Manitoba to Cleveland to be close to their children. They have four children and seven grandchildren. They have become leaders in the Jewish community. Lena sees her brother Avrum at least three times a week.

Avrum and his wife Mollie have three children and eight grandchildren. Their happiness is enhanced by Avrum finding his sister, Lena. He is a regular lecturer at schools and social organizations, speaking about the Holocaust.

Both Avrum's and Lena's children, and grandchildren, can sing the song, "Little child, little child," passed on to them from childhood days.

ACKNOWLEDGMENTS

I wish to thank my brother, Arthur, a professional writer and published author, for all the time, energy, and advice he gave me. This is a better book because of his involvement in this writing adventure.

I also want to thank my wife, Carol, who suffered through my many moods during the writing of this book.

ABOUT THE AUTHORS

Author David Twain spent many years in the pet supply business, from distributor and retailer to importer—which took him to China, England, Taiwan, Thailand, Vietnam, Malaysia, and Nepal. It was on these lengthy flights that David passed his time by writing poetry and short stories. He has written more than 350 poems and short stories, including magazine articles, three autobiographies, and two musical CDs with twenty original songs. An ardent student of Jewish history, he became interested in the lives of Holocaust survivors during his extensive research, which culminated in his writing *The Precious Few*.

Art Twain, younger brother of David, has written successfully for a living for 58 years. Art has written and produced over 3,000 radio and tv commercials, myriad jingles and music scores, and countless print materials. His awards include Clios, Emmy, AAF, One Show, and more. He helped the Gap go from one store to 500 stores with his marketing and advertising. Art wrote *Falling into the Gap*, the 724-page biography of Don Fisher, founder of the Gap stores. He organized, edited, and added his writing skills to *The Precious Few*.

AMSTERDAM PUBLISHERS HOLOCAUST LIBRARY

The series **Holocaust Survivor Memoirs World War II** consists of the following autobiographies of survivors:

Outcry. Holocaust Memoirs, by Manny Steinberg

Hank Brodt Holocaust Memoirs. A Candle and a Promise, by Deborah Donnelly

The Dead Years. Holocaust Memoirs, by Joseph Schupack

Rescued from the Ashes. The Diary of Leokadia Schmidt, Survivor of the Warsaw Ghetto, by Leokadia Schmidt

My Lvov. Holocaust Memoir of a twelve-year-old Girl, by Janina Hescheles

Remembering Ravensbrück. From Holocaust to Healing, by Natalie Hess

Wolf. A Story of Hate, by Zeev Scheinwald with Ella Scheinwald

Save my Children. An Astonishing Tale of Survival and its Unlikely Hero, by Leon Kleiner with Edwin Stepp

Holocaust Memoirs of a Bergen-Belsen Survivor & Classmate of Anne Frank, by Nanette Blitz Konig

Defiant German - Defiant Jew. A Holocaust Memoir from inside the Third Reich, by Walter Leopold with Les Leopold

In a Land of Forest and Darkness. The Holocaust Story of two Jewish Partisans, by Sara Lustigman Omelinski

Holocaust Memories. Annihilation and Survival in Slovakia, by Paul Davidovits

From Auschwitz with Love. The Inspiring Memoir of Two Sisters' Survival, Devotion and Triumph Told by Manci Grunberger Beran & Ruth Grunberger Mermelstein, by Daniel Seymour

Remetz. Resistance Fighter and Survivor of the Warsaw Ghetto, by Jan Yohay Remetz

My March Through Hell. A Young Girl's Terrifying Journey to Survival, by Halina Kleiner with Edwin Stepp

Roman's Journey, by Roman Halter

Memoirs by Elmar Rivosh, Sculptor (1906-1967). Riga Ghetto and Beyond, by Elmar Rivosh

The series **Holocaust Survivor True Stories WWII** consists of the following biographies:

Among the Reeds. The true story of how a family survived the Holocaust, by Tammy Bottner

A Holocaust Memoir of Love & Resilience. Mama's Survival from Lithuania to America, by Ettie Zilber

Living among the Dead. My Grandmother's Holocaust Survival Story of Love and Strength, by Adena Bernstein Astrowsky

Heart Songs. A Holocaust Memoir, by Barbara Gilford

Shoes of the Shoah. The Tomorrow of Yesterday, by Dorothy Pierce

Hidden in Berlin. A Holocaust Memoir, by Evelyn Joseph Grossman

Separated Together. The Incredible True WWII Story of Soulmates Stranded an Ocean Apart, by Kenneth P. Price, Ph.D.

The Man Across the River. The incredible story of one man's will to survive the Holocaust, by Zvi Wiesenfeld

If Anyone Calls, Tell Them I Died. A Memoir, by Emanuel (Manu) Rosen

The House on Thrömerstrasse. A Story of Rebirth and Renewal in the Wake of the Holocaust, by Ron Vincent

Dancing with my Father. His hidden past. Her quest for truth. How Nazi Vienna shaped a family's identity, by Jo Sorochinsky

The Story Keeper. Weaving the Threads of Time and Memory - A Memoir, by Fred Feldman

Krisia's Silence. The Girl who was not on Schindler's List, by Ronny Hein

Defying Death on the Danube. A Holocaust Survival Story, by Debbie J. Callahan with Henry Stern

A Doorway to Heroism. A decorated German-Jewish Soldier who became an American Hero, by Rabbi W. Jack Romberg

The Shoemaker's Son. The Life of a Holocaust Resister, by Laura Beth Bakst

The Redhead of Auschwitz. A True Story, by Nechama Birnbaum

Land of Many Bridges. My Father's Story, by Bela Ruth Samuel Tenenholtz

Creating Beauty from the Abyss. The Amazing Story of Sam Herciger, Auschwitz Survivor and Artist, by Lesley Ann Richardson

On Sunny Days We Sang. A Holocaust Story of Survival and Resilience, by Jeannette Grunhaus de Gelman

Painful Joy. A Holocaust Family Memoir, by Max J. Friedman

I Give You My Heart. A True Story of Courage and Survival, by Wendy Holden

In the Time of Madmen, by Mark A. Prelas

Monsters and Miracles. Horror, Heroes and the Holocaust, by Ira Wesley Kitmacher

Flower of Vlora. Growing up Jewish in Communist Albania, by Anna Kohen

Aftermath: Coming of Age on Three Continents. A Memoir, by Annette Libeskind Berkovits

Not a real Enemy. The True Story of a Hungarian Jewish Man's Fight for Freedom, by Robert Wolf

Zaidy's War. Four Armies, Three Continents, Two Brothers. One Man's Impossible Story of Endurance, by Martin Bodek

The Glassmaker's Son. Looking for the World my Father left behind in Nazi Germany, by Peter Kupfer

The Apprentice of Buchenwald. The True Story of the Teenage Boy Who Sabotaged Hitler's War Machine, by Oren Schneider

Good for a Single Journey, by Helen Joyce

Burying the Ghosts, by Sonia Case

American Wolf. From Nazi Refugee to American Spy. A True Story, by Audrey Birnbaum

Bipolar Refugee. A Saga of Survival and Resilience, by Peter Wiesner

The series **Jewish Children in the Holocaust** consists of the following autobiographies of Jewish children hidden during WWII in the Netherlands:

Searching for Home. The Impact of WWII on a Hidden Child, by Joseph Gosler

See You Tonight and Promise to be a Good Boy! War memories, by Salo Muller

Sounds from Silence. Reflections of a Child Holocaust Survivor, Psychiatrist and Teacher, by Robert Krell

Sabine's Odyssey. A Hidden Child and her Dutch Rescuers, by Agnes Schipper

The Journey of a Hidden Child, by Harry Pila and Robin Black

The series **New Jewish Fiction** consists of the following novels, written by Jewish authors. All novels are set in the time during or after the Holocaust.

The Corset Maker. A Novel, by Annette Libeskind Berkovits

Escaping the Whale. The Holocaust is over. But is it ever over for the next generation? by Ruth Rotkowitz

When the Music Stopped. Willy Rosen's Holocaust, by Casey Hayes

Hands of Gold. One Man's Quest to Find the Silver Lining in Misfortune, by Roni Robbins

The Girl Who Counted Numbers. A Novel, by Roslyn Bernstein

There was a garden in Nuremberg. A Novel, by Navina Michal Clemerson

The Butterfly and the Axe, by Omer Bartov

To Live Another Day. A Novel, Elizabeth Rosenberg

A Worthy Life. A Novel, by Dahlia Moore

The series **Holocaust Heritage** consists of the following memoirs by 2G:

The Cello Still Sings. A Generational Story of the Holocaust and of the Transformative Power of Music, by Janet Horvath

The Fire and the Bonfire. A Journey into Memory, by Ardyn Halter

The Silk Factory: Finding Threads of My Family's True Holocaust Story, by Michael Hickins

The series **Holocaust Books for Young Adults** consists of the following novels, based on true stories:

The Boy behind the Door. How Salomon Kool Escaped the Nazis. Inspired by a True Story, by David Tabatsky

Running for Shelter. A True Story, by Suzette Sheft

The Precious Few. An Inspirational Saga of Courage based on True Stories, by David Twain with Art Twain

The series **WW2 Historical Fiction** consists of the following novels, some of which are based on true stories:

Mendelevski's Box. A Heartwarming and Heartbreaking Jewish Survivor's Story, by Roger Swindells

A Quiet Genocide. The Untold Holocaust of Disabled Children WW2 Germany, by Glenn Bryant

The Knife-Edge Path, by Patrick T. Leahy

Brave Face. The Inspiring WWII Memoir of a Dutch/German Child, by I. Caroline Crocker and Meta A. Evenbly

When We Had Wings. The Gripping Story of an Orphan in Janusz Korczak's Orphanage. A Historical Novel, by Tami Shem-Tov

Jacob's Courage: A Holocaust Love Story, by Charles S. Weinblatt

Want to be an AP book reviewer?

Reviews are very important in a world dominated by the social media and social proof. Please drop us a line if you want to join the *AP review team* and show us at least one review already posted on Amazon for one of our books.

info@amsterdampublishers.com

www.ingramcontent.com/pod-product-compliance
Lightning Source LLC
LaVergne TN
LVHW091547070526
838199LV00024B/565/J